THE ENGLISH MADRIGAL SCHOOL

Transcribed, Scored and Edited by

REV. EDMUND HORACE FELLOWES

M.A., Mus.Doc.

VOL. XXIII.

JOHN BENNET

MADRIGALS TO FOUR VOICES

(Published in 1599)

A MADRIGAL by JOHN BENNET

(Included by Morley in the "Triumphs of Oriana," published in 1601)

TWO SONGS OF FOUR PARTS by JOHN BENNET

(Included by Thomas Ravenscroft in his "Brief Discourse," published in 1614)

LONDON:
STAINER AND BELL, LTD.,
69 NEWMAN STREET, OXFORD STREET, W.

1922.

PREFACE TO VOL. XXIII.

IT has not been thought necessary to reprint in each volume of this Series the full explanation of the methods adopted by the Editor, especially as the Preface to Volume I. is published separately, and can be obtained separately by those who have not a copy of that volume. It is very important, however, to emphasize that a thorough grasp of the principles which are explained in detail in that treatise is absolutely indispensable for a clear understanding and practical use of this Edition, and particular attention is directed to the paragraph on Rhythm and Barring.

The musical illustrations there employed are drawn exclusively from the works of Thomas Morley, but the principles which they illustrate apply to the whole of this Series.

The following points are fully dealt with under separate headings:—

1. Clefs.
2. Words.
3. Expression.
4. Rhythm and Barring.
5. Repeat Marks.
6. Time-signatures.
7. Key-signatures.
8. Accidentals.
9. Pianoforte Score.

Though I have used every endeavour to reproduce an accurate version of the original text throughout this Series, I am aware that in a work of this magnitude it is almost inevitable that some misprints should escape detection in reading the proofs. I shall be glad to have any such misprints brought to my notice, so that they may be corrected in future editions. I shall also welcome any information as to the authorship of any of the lyrics not hitherto identified.

Nothing is known of Bennet's personal history. The dedication of his set of madrigals to Ralph Assheton points to his connexion with the borders of Cheshire and Lancashire, a district associated with two other madrigalists, Bateson and Pilkington.

The present Volume contains the Set of four-part madrigals published in 1599 and also Bennet's very gay contribution to the "Triumphs of Oriana." In addition to these, this Volume contains two of this composer's songs included by Ravenscroft in his "Brief Discourse." The other four of Bennet's songs in Ravenscroft's book are not in any sense madrigalian, being solo-songs or duets with chorus, and for that reason they are not reproduced here.

It will be noticed that comparatively few of Bennet's madrigals are for the usual S.A.T.B. scheme. Some of them offer opportunities for unusual combinations of voices; several numbers are within the range of female voices, whie some can be transposed for male voices alone.

EDMUND H. FELLOWES.

THE CLOISTERS,
WINDSOR CASTLE.
March 10th, 1918.

LYRICS

SET TO MUSIC BY

JOHN BENNET

In his Madrigals to four voices.

I.

I wander up and down and fain would rest me,
Yet cannot rest, such cares do still molest me.
All things conspire, I see, and this consent in
To find a place for me fit to lament in.

II.

Weep, silly soul disdained,
Thy helpless hap lamenting
That Love, whose passion pained
Wrought never thy contenting.
And since thou art disdained,
By them thou most affected,
Let them now be rejected.

III.

So gracious is thy sweet self, so fair, so framed
That whoso sees thee without a heart enflamed
Either he lives not or love's delight he knows not.

IV.

Let go, let go! why do you stay me?
I will for spite go run and slay me.
O new-found tormenting, O strange disdaining!
I die for love, yet feigned is my complaining.
But you that say I feigned
Now see what you have gained.
I will for spite go run and slay me;
Let go, let go! why do you stay me?

V.

Come, shepherds, follow me,
Run up apace the mountain
See, lo, besides the fountain
Love laid to rest how sweetly sleepeth he.
O take heed, come not nigh him
But haste we hence and fly him,
And, lovers, dance with gladness
For while Love sleeps is truce with care and sadness.

VI.

I languish to complain me with ghastly grief tormented;
I stand amazed to see you discontented.
Better I hold my peace and stop my breath
Than cause my sorrows to increase and work my death.

VII.

Sing out, ye nymphs and shepherds of Parnassus,
With sweet delight your merry notes consenting,
Sith time affords to banish love relenting,
Fortune she smiles sweetly still to grace us.

VIII.

Thrysis, sleepest thou? Holla! Let not sorrow slay us.
Hold up thy head, man, said the gentle Melibœus.
See Summer comes again the country's pride adorning,
Hark how the cuckoo singeth this fair April morning.
O, said the shepherd, and sighed as one all undone,
Let me alone, alas, and drive him back to London.

IX.

Ye restless thoughts, that harbour discontent,
Cease your assaults, and let my heart lament,
And let my tongue have leave to tell my grief,
That she may pity, though not grant relief.
Pity would help what Love hath almost slain
And salve the wound that festered this disdain.

X.

Whenas I glance on my sweet lovely Phyllis,
Whose cheeks are decked with roses and with lilies,
I me complain that me she nought regarded
And that my love with envy was rewarded.
Then wantonly she smileth
And grief from me exileth.

XI.

Cruel unkind, my heart thou hast bereft me
And will not leave while any life is left me;
And yet still will I love thee.

XII.

O sleep, fond Fancy, sleep! my head thou tirest
With false delight of that which thou desirest.
Sleep, sleep, I say, and leave my thoughts molesting,
Thy master's head hath need of sleep and resting.

XIII.

Weep, O mine eyes, and cease not;
These your spring-tides, alas, methinks increase not.
O when, O when begin you
To swell so high that I may drown me in you?

XIV.

Since neither tunes of joy nor notes of sadness,
Cruel unkind, can move thee,
I will go run away for rage and madness
Because I will not love thee.
O come again, thy fruitless labour waste not.
How wilt thou run, fool, when thy heart thou hast not?

XV.

O grief! where shall poor Grief find patient hearing?
Footsteps of men I fly, my paths each creature baulking.
Wild and unhaunted woods seem tired with my walking.
Earth with my tears are drunk, air with my sighs tormented,
Heavens with my crying grown deaf and discontented,
Infernal cares affrighted with my doleful accenting;
Only my love loves my lamenting.

XVI.

O sweet grief, O sweet sighs, O sweet disdaining;
O sweet repulses, sweet wrongs, sweet lamenting,
Words sharply sweet and sweetly sharp consenting;
O sweet unkindness, sweet fears, sweet complaining.
Grieve then no more, my soul, those deep groans straining.
Your bitter anguish now shall have relenting
And sharp disdains receive their full contenting.

XVII.

Rest now, Amphion, rest thy charming lyre,
For Daphne's love, sweet love, makes melody.
Her love's concord with mine doth well conspire,
No discord jars in our love's sympathy.
Our concords have some discords mixed among;
Discording concords makes the sweetest song.

From "THE TRIUMPHS OF ORIANA."

All creatures now are merry merry minded,
The shepherds' daughters playing,
The nymphs are fa-la-laing.
Yond bugle was well winded.
At Orianaes presence each thing smileth,
The flowers themselves discover,
Birds over her do hover,
Music the time beguileth.
See where she comes with flowery garlands crowned
Queen of all queens renowned.
Then sang the shepherds and nymphs of Diana:
Long live fair Oriana.

From RAVENSCROFT'S "BRIEF DISCOURSE."

No. 5. Hawking for the Heron and Duck.

Lure, falconers! give warning to the field.
Let fly! let fly! make mounting herons to yield.
Die, fearful ducks, and climb no more so high,
The nyas-hawk will kiss the azure sky.
But when our soar-hawks fly and stiff winds blow,
Then long too late we falconers cry Hey lo!

No. 9. The Elves Dance.

Round about, round about
In a fair ring a,
Thus we dance, thus we dance,
And thus we sing a.
Trip and go, to and fro
Over this green a,
All about, in and out
Over this green a.

NOTES

III.—These words are a translation of Feretti's madrigal ***Sei tanto gratiosa*** in Yonge's Musica Transalpina (1st Set, No. 25.)

V.—Compare Morley's " Come, lovers, follow me." (See Vol. II., No. 11.)

VI.—These lines are a translation of a madrigal by Ferrabosco printed in Morley's 1598 Italian collection.

XI.—A translation of *Donna crudel,* another of Feretti's madrigals in Musica Transalpina (1st Set, No. 26).

XII.—Morley wrote a canzonet to these words which he printed among the examples in his " Plain and Easy Introduction to Practical Music."

XV. and XVI.—There is no indication in the part-books that these two poems are part of one whole, and yet they have all the appearance of being connected. It is possible, allowing for several textual alterations in the first section, that the poem was originally in sonnet-form.

XVII.—Line 1. *Amphion.* The son of Zeus and Antiope. He was the musician to the sound of whose lyre dead stones built themselves up as the walls of Thebes.

Hawking Song.

Line 1. *lure.* Spelt *luer* in the original edition and evidently pronounced in two syllables. The lure was an apparatus used by falconers to recall their hawks. It was constructed of a bunch of feathers to which a long cord or thong was attached. The intransitive verb, as used here, means to call to a hawk while casting the lure.

Line 4. *nyas-hawk.* A corrupted form of *eyas-hawk,* a technical term for a hawk brought up under a buzzard.

Line 6. *soar-hawks.* Another technical term in hawking and applied to a first-year bird.

Line 6. *stiff.* The Tenor part has the variant *swift.*

The Elves' Dance.

These words are from the " Maid's Metamorphosis " (Act II.), a play sometimes, but without any real evidence, attributed to Lyly.

MADRIGALLS

TO

FOVRE VOYCES

NEWLY PVBLISHED

BY

IOHN BENNET

HIS

FIRST WORKS

AT LONDON

Printed in little Saint Hellens by *William Barley, the Aſsigne of* Thomas Morley.

Cvm Priuilegio

MD.XC.IX.

TO THE RIGHT WORSHIPFVL,

RALPH ASSHETON Eſq : one of her Maieſties
Juſtices of Peace, and Quorum : and of the Oier
and terminer in the County Palantine of Lancaster and
Receiuer of her highneſſe Duchy reuenues, in the ſaid
County : and the Countie Palantine of Cheſter.

Right worſhipfull, It would be too tedious to make particuler declaration of your worſhipfull fauours, from time to time, towards me. I hauing beene hitherto altogether vnable, so much as to make any ſhow of thankfulnes for the same. And ſeeing it hath pleaſed GOD to make you, many waies a principall patron of my good : by meanes whereof, I haue at length attained to ſomwhat, whereby I may manifeſt my ſelfe, a well affected member of the common wealth. I haue thought it my duetie, to preſent vnto your worſhip, theſe firſt fruits of my ſimple skill. Beſeeching you, fauourablie to accept them, as the indeauors of a yong wit, and tokens of a thankfull mind. And becauſe I haue alwaies knowne you a fauourer of all good exerciſes, and namely of Musicke : I am imbouldned to craue your worſhipfull Patronage of theſe my labours; whereby I shall be incouraged, to indeauor my ſelfe with all diligence, to put in practiſe ſome others, that may deſerue better acceptation. Thus leauing them to your delightfull recreation, and your worſhip to the protection of the moſt high, I humbly take my leaue.

Your worſhips in all duetie,

Iohn Bennet.

TABLE OF CONTENTS

A MADRIGAL FROM THE "TRIUMPHS OF ORIANA."

TWO SONGS OF FOUR PARTS FROM RAVENSCROFT'S "BRIEF DISCOURSE."

John Bennet's Madrigals

TO

Four Voices.

(1599)

Edited by EDMUND H. FELLOWES.

Nº 1. I WANDER UP AND DOWN.

* The single low D may be taken an octave higher if female voices are employed.

 S. & B. 2375.

and fain would rest me, and fain would
me, and fain would rest me, and fain would rest
fain would rest me, and fain would rest me,
rest me, rest me,
rest me, and fain would rest me, rest
me, and fain, and fain would rest me, and fain would rest
and fain would rest me, and fain would rest
and fain would rest me, and fain would rest
p
me, Yet can-not rest, yet can-not rest, such cares do
me, Yet can-not rest, yet can-not rest, such
me, Yet can-not rest, yet can - not rest, yet can-not
me, Yet can-not rest, yet can-not rest, such
f

still mo - lest me, yet can - not rest,
cares do still mo - lest me, yet can - not
rest, such cares do still mo - lest me, yet
cares do still mo - lest me, yet can - not
yet can - not rest, such cares do still mo - lest
rest, yet can - not rest, such cares do
can - not rest, yet can - not rest, such cares do
rest, yet can - not rest, such cares do still mo -
mf
me, All things con - spire I
still mo - lest me, All things con - spire I
still mo - lest me, All things con - spire I see, I see, all
-lest, me, All things con - spire I see, all

see, all things con-spire I see, and this con-sent
see, con-spire I see, and this con-sent, and this, and
things con-spire I see, con - spire I see, and this
things con-spire I see, and this con-sent in, and
in, con-sent in, To find a
this con-sent in, To find a place for me,
con-sent in, To find a place for
this con-sent in, To find a place for me, to
place for me, a place for me, to find a
to find a place for me, to
me, for me, to find a place for me,
find a place for me, to find a place for me, to

place for me, for me fit to la - ment, fit
find a place for me, for me fit to la -
for me fit to la -
find a place for me, for me fit to la - ment, fit
p
to la - ment, a place for me fit
-ment in, fit to la - ment, for me
-ment in, fit to la - ment in, fit
to la - ment in, for me fit
to la - ment, to la - ment in.
fit to la - ment in.
to la - ment in.
to la - ment in.

Nº 2. WEEP, SILLY SOUL DISDAINED.

Copyright, 1922, in U.S.A. by Stainer & Bell Ltd.

f
soul dis - dain - ed. Thy hap - less hap, thy hap - less
since thou art, and since thou
soul dis - dain - ed. Thy hap - less hap, thy
And since thou art, and
f
-dain - - ed. Thy hap - less hap, thy
And since thou art, and
f
-dain - - ed. Thy hap - less hap, thy
And since thou art, and
f
hap la - ment - ing, la - ment - ing, thy
art dis - dain - ed, dis - dain - ed, and
hap - less hap la - ment - ing, la - ment - ing,
since thou art dis - dain - ed, dis - dain - ed,
hap - less hap la - ment - ing, la - ment - ing, thy hap - less
since thou art dis - dain - ed, dis - dain - ed, and since thou
hap - less hap la - ment - ing, That
since thou art dis - dain - ed, by

hap - less hap la - ment - ing, That
since thou art dis - dain - ed, by
That love whose pas - sion pain - -
by them thou most af - fect - -
hap la - ment - ing, That love whose pas - sion
art dis - dain - ed, by them thou most af -
love whose pas - sion pain - - - ed,
them thou most af - fect - - ed,
p
love whose pas - sion pain - ed, wrought
them thou most af - fect - ed, Let
-ed, that love whose pas - sion pain - -
-ed, by them thou most af - fect - -
pain - - ed, wrought nev - er thy con - tent -
- fect - - ed, thou most af - fect -
p
pain - - - ed, that
af - - fect - ed, by
p

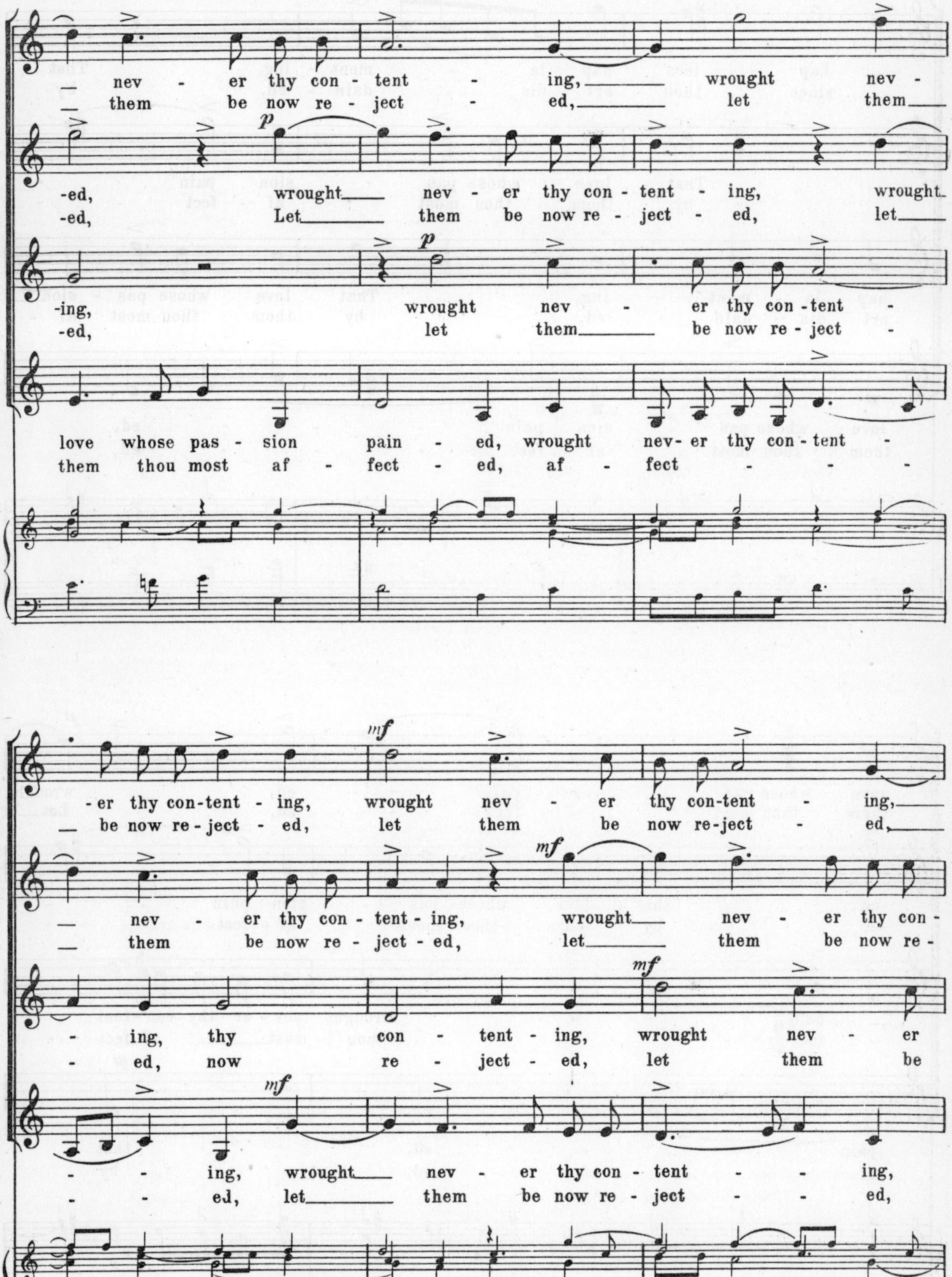
nev - er thy con tent - ing, wrought nev -
them be now re - ject - ed, let them
-ed, wrought nev - er thy con - tent - ing, wrought
-ed, Let them be now re - ject - ed, let
-ing, wrought nev - er thy con - tent -
-ed, let them be now re - ject -
love whose pas - sion pain - ed, wrought nev - er thy con - tent -
them thou most af - fect - ed, af - fect - - -
p
- er thy con - tent - ing, wrought nev - er thy con - tent - ing,
be now re - ject - ed, let them be now re - ject - ed,
nev - er thy con - tent - ing, wrought nev - er thy con -
them be now re - ject - ed, let them be now re -
- ing, thy con - tent - ing, wrought nev - er
- ed, now re - ject - ed, let them be
- - ing, wrought nev - er thy con - tent - - - ing,
- - ed, let them be now re - ject - - - ed,
mf

thy con-tent - ing, wrought nev - er thy con-tent -
now re-ject - ed, let them be now re-ject -
-tent - ing, thy con -
-ject - ed, now re -
thy con-tent - ing, wrought nev-er thy con-tent -
now re - ject - ed, let them be now re - ject -
wrought nev - er thy con-tent - ing,
let them be now re-ject - ed,
-ing, wrought nev - er thy con-tent - ing, wrought
-ed, let them be now re-ject - ed, let
-tent - ing, wrought nev - er thy con-tent -
-ject - ed, let them be now re-ject -
- - ing, wrought nev - er thy con -
- - ed, let them be now re -
wrought nev-er thy con-tent - ing, con-tent - ing,
let them be now re-ject - ed, re-ject - ed,
p
mf
p

✻ In this repeat the Cantus and Altus interchange parts.

Nº 3. SO GRACIOUS IS THY SWEET SELF.

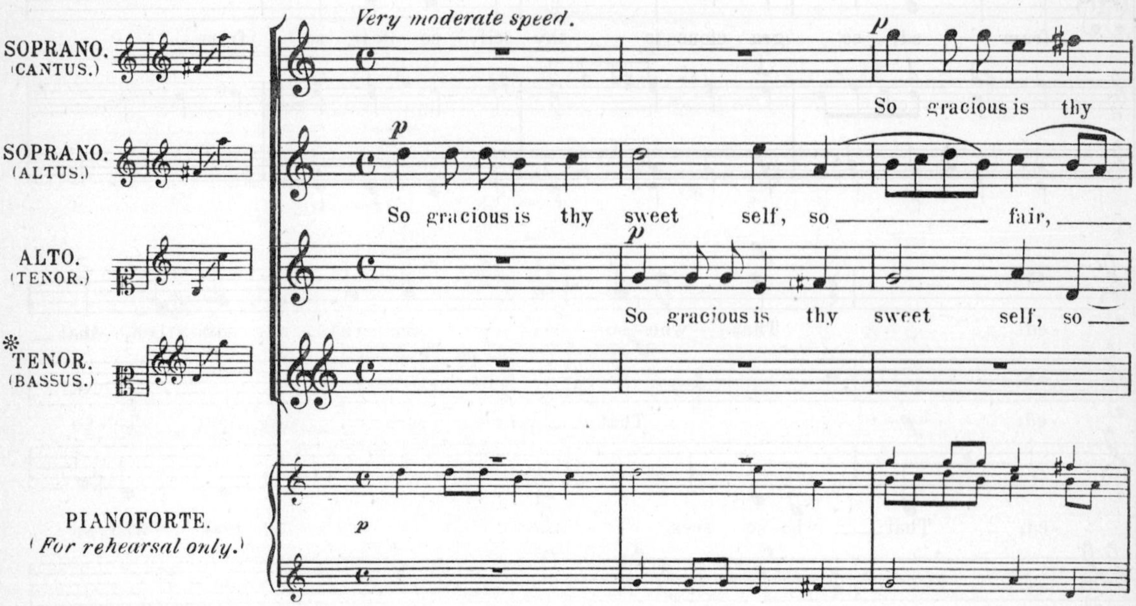

*If the one low D is taken an octave higher, this part can be sung by female voices.

self, so fair, so fram-ed, so fair, so fram- - -
is thy sweet self, so fair, so fram-
self, so fair, so gra-cious is thy sweet self, so fair, so fram-
fram-ed, so gra-cious is thy self, so fair, so fram-
-ed. That who-so sees thee, who-so sees thee, that
-ed: That who-so sees thee, that who-so
-ed: That who-so sees thee, that who-so
-ed: That who-so sees thee, who-so sees
who-so sees thee, that who-so sees thee with-
sees thee with-out a heart en-flam-ed, with-
sees thee, who-so sees thee with-out a
thee, that who-so sees thee with-out a heart en-

-out a heart en - - - flam - ed, with - out a heart en - -
-out a heart en - flam - ed, with - out a heart en -
heart en - flam - ed, with - out a heart en - flam - ed,
- flam - ed, with - out a heart en - - flam - ed,
-flam - ed, with - out a heart en - flam - ed, Ei -
- - flam - - - - - ed, Ei -
with - out a heart en - - - flam - - - ed, Ei -
with - out a heart en - flam - ed,
p
- ther he lives not, ei - ther he lives not, ei - ther he lives
- ther he lives not, ei - ther he lives not,
- ther he lives not, ei - ther he lives not, ei - ther he
ei - ther he lives not, ei -
p

*In this repeat the Cantus and Altus interchange parts.

Nº 4. LET GO! WHY DO YOU STAY ME?

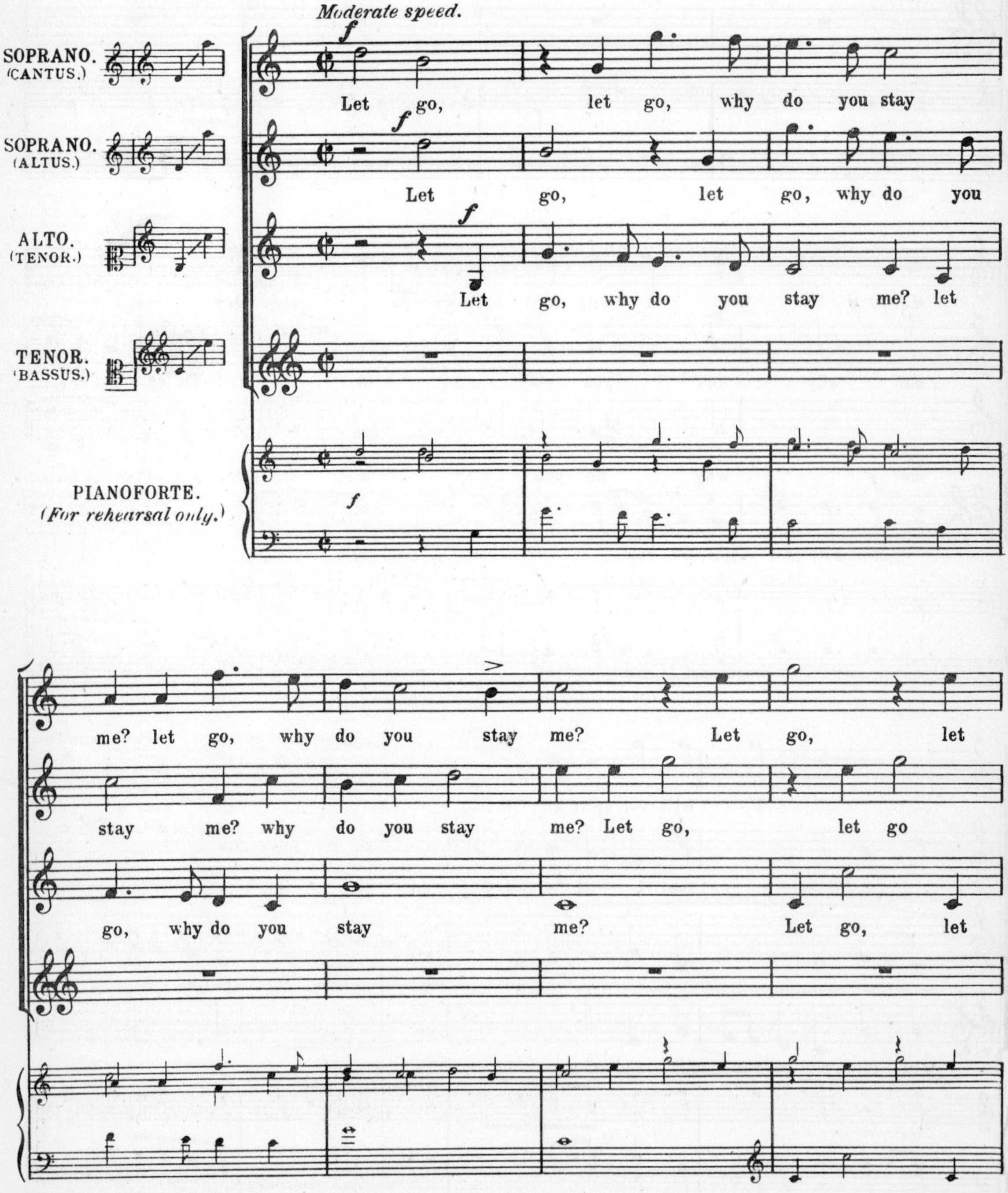

go, let go, let go, let go, why do you stay
let go, let go, let go, let go, let go, why do you stay
go, let go, let go, let go, why do you stay
me? I will for spite go run and slay me,
me? why do you stay me? I will for spite go run
me? why do you stay me? why do you stay
f
I will for spite go run and slay me, I
I will for spite go run and slay me, go run
and slay me, I will for spite go run and slay me, I will for
me? I will for spite go run and
will for spite go run and slay me,

and slay me, go run
spite go run and slay me, I will for spite go run and
slay me. I will for spite go run and slay
I will for spite go run and slay me, go run and
and slay me. O new
slay me. O new found tor - ment -
me, and slay me. O new found tor - ment -
slay me. O new found tor - ment -
found tor - ment - ing, O strange dis -
- ing, new found tor-ment - ing, O strange dis - dain -
- ing, new found tor - ment - ing, O strange dis -
- ing, new found tor - ment - ing, O strange dis -

-dain - ing. I die for love, for love, I die for love, I die for
- ing. I die for love, for love, I die for love, I die for
-dain - ing. I die for love, I die for love, for
-dain - ing. I die for love, I die for love,
mf
love, yet feigned is my complain - ing: But you that say I
love, yet feigned is my com - plain - ing: But you that say I
love, yet feigned is my com - plain - ing: But you that say I
yet feigned is my com - plain - ing:
p
cresc.
f
feign - ed, now see what you have gain - ed, now
feign - ed, now see what you have gain - ed,
feign - ed, now see what you have gain - ed, now
Now see what you have gain - ed, I will for
p cresc.

see what you have gain - ed, I will for spite go run
I will for spite go run and slay me,
see what you have gain - ed, now see what you
spite go run and slay me, I
and slay me, I will for spite go run and slay
I will for spite go run and
have gain - - ed, I will for
will for spite go run and slay me,
me, I will for spite go run and slay me, I
slay me, go run and
spite go run and slay me, I will for
I will for spite go run and

will for spite go run and slay
slay me, go run and slay
spite go run and slay
slay me, go run and slay
me. Let go, let go, let go, let go, let
me. Let go, let go, let go, let go,
me. Let go, let go, let go, why do you
me. Let go, let
go, let go, let go, why do you stay me?
let go, let go, why do you stay me?
stay me? let go, why do you stay me?
go, let go, let go, why do you stay me?

Nº 5. COME, SHEPHERDS, FOLLOW ME.

- - ain,
- ain, come, shep - herds,
shep - herds, fol - low me, run up a - pace the mount - ain,
Come, shep - herds, fol - low me, run
run up a - pace the mount - ain, run up a - pace the mount -
shep - herds, fol - low me, run up a - pace the mount -
run up a - pace the mount -
up a - pace the mount - ain, run up a - pace the mount -
- ain, See lo, see lo, see lo, be - sides the
- ain, See lo, be - sides the fount - ain, see
- ain, See lo, see lo, be - sides, be - sides the
- ain, See lo, see lo, see lo, be -

mf
fount - ain, see lo, be - sides, be - sides, see lo, be -
lo be - sides, see lo, be - sides the fount - ain,
fount - ain, see lo, be - sides the fount - ain, be -
- sides the fount - ain, see lo, be -
p
pp
- sides the fount - ain, Love laid to rest, How
Love laid to rest, to rest, How
- sides the fount - ain, Love laid to rest, to rest, How
- sides the fount - ain, Love laid to rest,
sweet - ly, sweet - ly sleep - eth
sweet - ly, sweet ly sleep - eth he, how sweet - ly,
sweet - ly sweet - ly sleep - eth

he, how sweet - ly, sweet - ly sleep -
sweet - ly sleep - eth he, how
he, how sweet - ly, sweet - ly sleep - - eth he, how
How sweet - ly, sweet - ly sleep - - -
- - eth he, how sweet - ly sleep - eth he. O
sweet - ly, sweet - ly sleep - eth he. O
sweet - ly sleep - eth he. O take heed, take
- eth he. O take heed come
take heed, come not nigh him, But haste we
take heed, come not nigh him, But haste we hence and fly
heed, come not nigh him, But haste we hence and fly
not nigh him, come not nigh him, But
cresc.
p

hence and fly him.
him, but haste we hence and fly him.
him, but haste we hence and fly him.
haste we hence and fly him.
(𝅗𝅥. = 𝅗𝅥) (𝅘𝅥 = 𝅗𝅥)
f
And lov - ers dance, and lov - ers dance with glad -
And lov - ers dance, and lov - ers dance, lov - ers
And lov - ers dance, and lov - ers dance with
And lov - ers dance, and lov - ers dance
- ness, with glad - ness, with glad - ness, with glad -
dance with glad - ness, with glad - ness, with
glad - ness, with glad - ness, with glad - ness
with glad - ness, with glad - ness,

p
-ness, with glad - ness, with glad - ness for
p
glad - ness, with glad - ness, glad - ness, for while Love
p
with glad - ness, for
p
with glad - ness, with glad - ness, for
p
f
while Love sleeps is
f
sleeps, for while Love sleeps, for while Love sleeps is truce with care
f
while Love sleeps, for while Love sleeps, for while Love sleeps is truce with
f
while Love sleeps, for while Love sleeps, for while Love sleeps is
f
truce with care and sad ness.
and sad - - ness.
care, is truce with care and sad - ness.
truce with care and sad - - ness.

Nº 6. I LANGUISH TO COMPLAIN ME.

com - plain me,
me, I lan - guish to com -
lan - guish to com - plain, to com - plain
I lan - - -
I lan - - guish to com -
-plain me, to com - plain
me, to
-guish to com - plain me, with
-plain me, with ghast - ly grief tor -
me, with ghast - ly grief tor - ment - ed, tor -
com - plain me, with ghast - ly grief tor -
ghast - ly grief tor - ment - -

p
-ment - - - - - ed, I stand
-ment - - - - - ed, I stand
-ment - - - - - ed, I stand
- - - - - - - ed, I stand
a - mazed, a - mazed to see you
a - mazed to see you, to see you
a - mazed to see you dis - con - tent -
a - mazed, a - mazed to see
dis - con - tent - ed, to see you dis - con -
dis - con - tent - ed, to see you dis - con - tent - -
- ed, dis - - con - tent - ed, dis - - con -
you dis - con - tent - ed, dis - con - tent - -

mf
-tent - ed. Bet - ter I hold
- - ed. Bet - ter I hold my peace, I
-tent - - ed. Bet - ter I hold my
-ed. Bet - ter I hold my peace,
p
my peace, and stop my breath,
hold my peace, and stop my
peace, and stop my breath,
and stop my breath,
Than cause my sor-rows to in - crease,
breath, Than cause my sor-rows to in-
Than cause my sor-rows to in-
Than cause my sor-rows to in - crease, than

than cause my sor-rows to in - crease,
- - crease, in-crease, in-crease, than cause
dim.
p
-crease, than cause my sor-rows to in - - - -
cause my sor-rows to in-crease, than cause my
p
p
than cause my sor-rows to in-crease, than cause
my sor-rows to in - crease, in-crease, than cause my sor-rows
-crease, than cause my sor - rows
sor-rows to in - - - crease, than cause my sor-rows to in-
my sor-rows to in-crease and work my death.
to in-crease and work my death.
to in-crease and work my death.
- - - - crease and work my death.

Nº 7. SING OUT, YE NYMPHS.

-sus, shep - herds of Par-nas - - - - - - sus, sing
of Par-nas - sus, sing out, ye Nymphs and shepherds of Par-nas -
Nymphs and shep-herds of Par - nas-sus, sing out, ye Nymphs and shepherds of Par - nas -
shep-herds of Par - nas - sus,
out, ye Nymphs and shep - herds of Par - - nas - sus, With
-sus, ye Nymphs and shep-herds of Par-nas - sus, shep - herds
-sus, sing out, ye Nymphs and shep-herds of Par - nas - sus, shep-herds
sing out, ye Nymphs and shep-herds of Par-nas - sus, With
dim.
sweet de-light your mer - - ry notes con - sent - -
p
of Par - nas - sus, With sweet de-light your mer - -
p
of Par - nas - sus, With sweet de-light your mer - ry
dim.
sweet de-light your mer - ry notes, your mer - ry notes con - sent -
p

p
-ing, with sweet de-light your mer - - - ry notes, your mer -
ry notes,
with sweet de-light your mer -
notes,
with sweet de-light your mer -
p
-ing, with sweet de-light your mer - - ry notes,
- - - ry notes con-sent - ing, con-sent - ing, Sith time af-
f
- - ry notes con - sent - - ing, Sith time af-
f
- ry notes con - sent - - ing, Sith time af-
f
your mer-ry notes con - sent - - ing, Sith time af-
f
f
-fords, to ban-ish love re-lent-ing, for-tune she smiles, for-tune she
-fords, to ban-ish love re-lent-ing, for-tune she smiles, for-tune she
-fords, to ban-ish love re-lent-ing, for-tune she smiles, for-tune she
-fords, to ban-ish love re-lent-ing, for-tune she smiles, for-tune she

* In this repeat the Cantus and Altus and the Tenor and Bassus, respectively, interchange parts.

Nº 8. THYRSIS, SLEEPEST THOU?

*E is perhaps a misprint for C.

f
p
— sum - mer comes a - gain, the coun - try's pride a - dorn - -
See sum - mer comes a - gain, the coun - try's
comes a - gain, the coun - try's pride a - dorn - - ing, see
See sum - mer comes a - gain, the coun - try's pride a - dorn -
ing, see sum - mer comes a - gain, the coun - try's pride a - dorn -
pride a - dorn - ing, see sum - mer comes a - gain, the
— sum - mer comes a - gain, the coun - try's pride a - dorn - ing, the
-ing, see sum - mer comes a - gain, the coun - try's
-ing, a - dorn - ing. cuc - koo, cuc - koo
coun - try's pride a - dorn - ing. Hark how the cuc - koo sing - eth,
— coun - try's pride a - dorn - ing. Hark how the cuc - koo sing -
pride a - dorn - ing. Hark how the cuc - koo sing - eth,

sing - eth, cuc - koo sing - eth, hark how the cuc - koo
cuc - koo sing eth, cuc - koo sing - eth, sing-
-eth, hark how the cuc - koo sing-eth, sing - eth, hark how the cuc - koo
hark how the cuc - koo sing - eth, hark how the cuc - koo sing-eth,
sing-eth, cuc - koo, this fair A - pril morn - ing, A - pril morn - ing.
- - eth, this fair A - pril morn - - ing. O
sing - - eth, this fair A - pril morn-ing. O said the
sing - - eth, this fair A - pril morn - ing. O
O said the shep - herd, and sighed as one all un -
said the shep-herd, and sighed, and sighed as one all un -
shep - herd, and sighed, and sighed as one
said the shep-herd, and sighed, and sighed as one all

cresc.
-done, Let me a-lone, a-las,
f
and drive him back to
cresc.
-done, un-done, Let me a-lone, a-las, and drive him back to
cresc.
all un-done, Let me a-lone, a-las, a-lone,
cresc.
un-done, Let me a-lone, a-las,
Lon-don, and drive him back to Lon-don, and drive him back to
Lon-don, and drive him back to Lon-don, and drive him back
a-las, and drive him back to
and drive him back to Lon-don, to Lon-
Lon-don, and drive him back to Lon-don and drive him back to Lon-don, to Lon-don.
to Lon-don, and drive him back to Lon-don, to Lon-don, to Lon-don.
Lon-don, and drive him back to London, to Lon-don.
-don, and drive him back to Lon-don, to Lon-don.

Nº 9. YE RESTLESS THOUGHTS.

-tent, dis - con - tent, that har -
-tent, that har-bour dis - con-tent, that har-bour dis - -
that har - bour dis - con-tent, that har - bour dis-con-tent,
-tent, that har - bour dis - con - tent, dis - - -
p
- bour dis - con - - tent, cease
p
- - con - - - tent, cease your as -
p
that har - bour dis - con - tent, cease your as-saults,
p
- - con - - - tent, cease your as-saults,
p
your as-saults and let my heart la - ment, and let my heart la -
-saults, as - saults, and let my heart la - ment, and let my heart la -
cease your as - saults, and let my heart la - ment, and
cease your as - saults, and let my heart la - ment, and

-ment, la - ment, And let my tongue have leave
- ment, la ment, And let my tongue, and let my tongue
let my heart la - ment, And let my tongue
let my heart la - ment, And let my tongue have
to tell my grief,
have leave to tell my grief, that
have leave to tell my grief, that she may pi - ty,
leave to tell my grief, that she may pi - ty,
mf
that she may pi - ty, though not grant re - lief, that she may
she may pi - ty, though not grant re - lief, that she may
though not grant re - lief, re - lief, that she may pi - ty though not
though not grant re - lief, that she may pi - ty though not grant re -

p
pi - ty, though not grant re - lief, Pi - ty would
pi - ty, though not grant re-lief, Pi - ty would help a - las, pi -
grant re - lief, re - lief, Pi - ty would help a - las,
- lief, re - lief, Pi - ty would
mf
help a - las, what love hath
- ty would help a - las, what love hath al - most
what love hath al - most slain,
help a - las, what love hath al - most
al - most slain, al - most slain,
slain, what love hath al - most
what love hath al - most slain,
slain, what love hath al - most slain, what

hath al - most slain, and
slain, hath al - most slain, and salve the wound that
hath al - most slain, and salve the wound that
love hath al - most slain, and
salve the wound that fest - ered this dis - dain, this dis -
fest - ered this dis - dain that
fest - ered this dis - dain, this dis -
salve the wound that fest - ered this dis - dain, that fest - ered this dis -
-dain, that fest - ered this dis - dain.
fest - ered this dis - dain.
-dain, that fest - ered this dis - dain.
-dain, that fest - ered this dis - dain.
p
mf

Nº 10. WHENAS I GLANCE.

*This will come within the compass of female voices if for the single low D the octave is substituted.

my love - ly Phyl - lis, Whose cheeks are decked with
my love - ly Phyl - lis, Whose cheeks are decked with
- ly Phil - lis, Whose cheeks are decked with
Phil - - lis, Whose cheeks are decked with
1.
p
Ros - es and Li - lies, When - as I
Ros - es and with Li - lies,
Ros - es, with Ros - es and Li - lies, When - as I glance on
Ros - es and Li - lies,
2.
CANTUS.
mf
- lies, I me com - plained,
ALTUS.
- lies, I me com -
- lies, I me com - plained, I me
- lies, I me com - plained, I me com -
mf

*In this repeat the Cantus and Altus interchange parts.

I me com - plained, that
-plained, I me com - plained, that
com - plained, I me com - plained, that
-plained, I me com - plained, that
she me nought re - gard - ed, And
she me nought re - gard - ed, And that my
she me nought re - gard - ed, And that my love with
she me nought re - gard - ed, And that my love with
that my love with en - vy was re - ward - ed. Then wan-ton-ly she
love with en - vy was re - ward - ed, re - ward - ed. Then wan-ton-ly she
en - vy was re - ward - ed, re - ward - ed.
en - vy was re - ward - ed, re - ward - ed.

* In this repeat the Cantus and Altus interchange parts.

Nº 11. CRUEL UNKIND.

p
hast be - reft me, Cru - el un - kind,
p
heart thou hast be - reft me, Cru - el un - kind,
p
heart thou hast be - reft me, my heart thou hast
p
hast be - reft me, Cru - el un -
p
my heart thou hast be - reft me, cru - el un -
cru - el un - kind, my heart thou hast
be - reft me, thou hast be - reft me, thou hast be -
-kind, my heart thou hast be - reft me,
-kind, my heart thou hast be - reft me, my
be - reft me, thou hast be - reft me my heart thou
-reft me, my heart thou hast be -
my heart thou hast be - reft me, my heart,

mf
heart, my heart thou hast be - reft me, And will not
hast be - reft me, thou hast be - reft me,
-reft, my heart thou hast be - reft me,
my heart thou hast be - reft me,
mf
leave, and will not leave while a - ny life is
mf
And will not leave, and will not leave while a - ny life is
mf
And will not leave while a - ny life is
mf
And will not leave, and will not leave while a - ny
p
left me, And yet, and yet, and yet,
p
left, is left me, And yet, and yet,
p
left, is left me, And yet, and yet, and
p
life is left me, And yet, and yet, and
p

— and yet, still will I love thee, And — yet, and —
and yet, still will I love thee, And yet, — and yet, —
yet, still will I love thee, And yet,
yet, still will I love thee, And yet, and
— yet, and — yet, still will I love thee.
— and yet, — and yet, still will I love thee.
and yet, and yet, still will I love thee.
yet, and yet, still will I love thee.

Nº 12. O SLEEP, FOND FANCY.

fan - cy, O sleep, O sleep, fond fan - cy,
fond fan - cy, O sleep, O sleep,
- cy, fond fan - cy, O sleep, O sleep, O sleep, fond fan -
fan - cy, O sleep, O sleep, fond fan -
O sleep, O sleep, fond fan - cy,
O sleep, O sleep, fond fan - cy,
- cy, O sleep, O sleep, fond fan - cy, O sleep, fond fan - cy, My
- cy, fond fan - cy, My
My head, a - las,
My head, a - las, thou tir - est,
head, a - las, a - las, thou tir -
head, a - las, thou tir - est, my
p
mf

— thou tir - est, my — head, a - las, — thou tir -
my head, a - las, thou tir - est, thou
- est, thou tir - est,
— head, a - las, — thou tir - est, thou tir - est,
- est, thou tir - est with false de -
tir - est, thou tir - est with false de -
thou tir - est with false de - light of that which thou de -
thou tir - est with false de - light of that which thou de -
- light of that which thou de - sir - est, of that which thou de - sir -
- light of that which thou de - sir - est, with false de - light of that which thou de - sir -
- sir - est, which thou de - sir - est, of that which thou de -
- sir - est, with false de - light of that which thou de - sir -

-est, of that, of that which thou de - sir -
-est, of that, of that which thou de - sir -
-sir - est, which thou de - sir - est, of that which thou de - sir -
-est, of that, of that which thou de - sir -
-est, Sleep, sleep, I say, fond fan -
-est, Sleep, sleep, I say, fond
-est, Sleep, sleep, I say, fond fan - cy, sleep, sleep, I
-est, Sleep, sleep, I say, fond fan - cy, sleep,
-cy, sleep, sleep, I say, fond fan - cy, And leave my
fan - cy, And leave my thoughts, and leave my
say, fond fan - cy, fond fan - cy, And leave my thoughts mo -
sleep, I say, fond fan - cy, And leave my thoughts mo - lest -

thoughts mo-lest - ing, thy mas-ter's head hath need of sleep and rest -
thoughts mo-lest - ing, thy mas - ter's
- lest - ing, thy mas - ter's head hath need of sleep, thy
-ing, mo-lest - ing, thy mas - ter's head hath need of sleep
-ing, hath need of sleep and rest - ing,
head hath need of sleep and rest - ing, sleep and rest -
mas - ter's head hath need of sleep and rest - ing, and rest -
and rest - ing, of rest -
hath need of sleep and rest - ing.
-ing, need of sleep and rest - ing.
-ing, need of sleep and rest - ing.
-ing, need of sleep and rest - ing.
pp

Nº 13. WEEP, O MINE EYES.

O mine eyes, and cease not,
weep O mine eyes and cease not, A - las,
eyes, weep O mine eyes and cease not, A -
eyes, weep and cease not, and cease
mf
mf
mf
mf
A - las, these your spring - tides a -
these your spring - tides a - las, these your
-las, these your spring tides a -
not, a - las, these your spring -
mf
-las, these your spring - tides me - thinks in - crease not.
spring - tides me-thinks in - crease not, me - thinks in - crease not.
-las, these your spring - tides me - thinks in - crease not.
-tides in - crease not, me - thinks in - crease not.

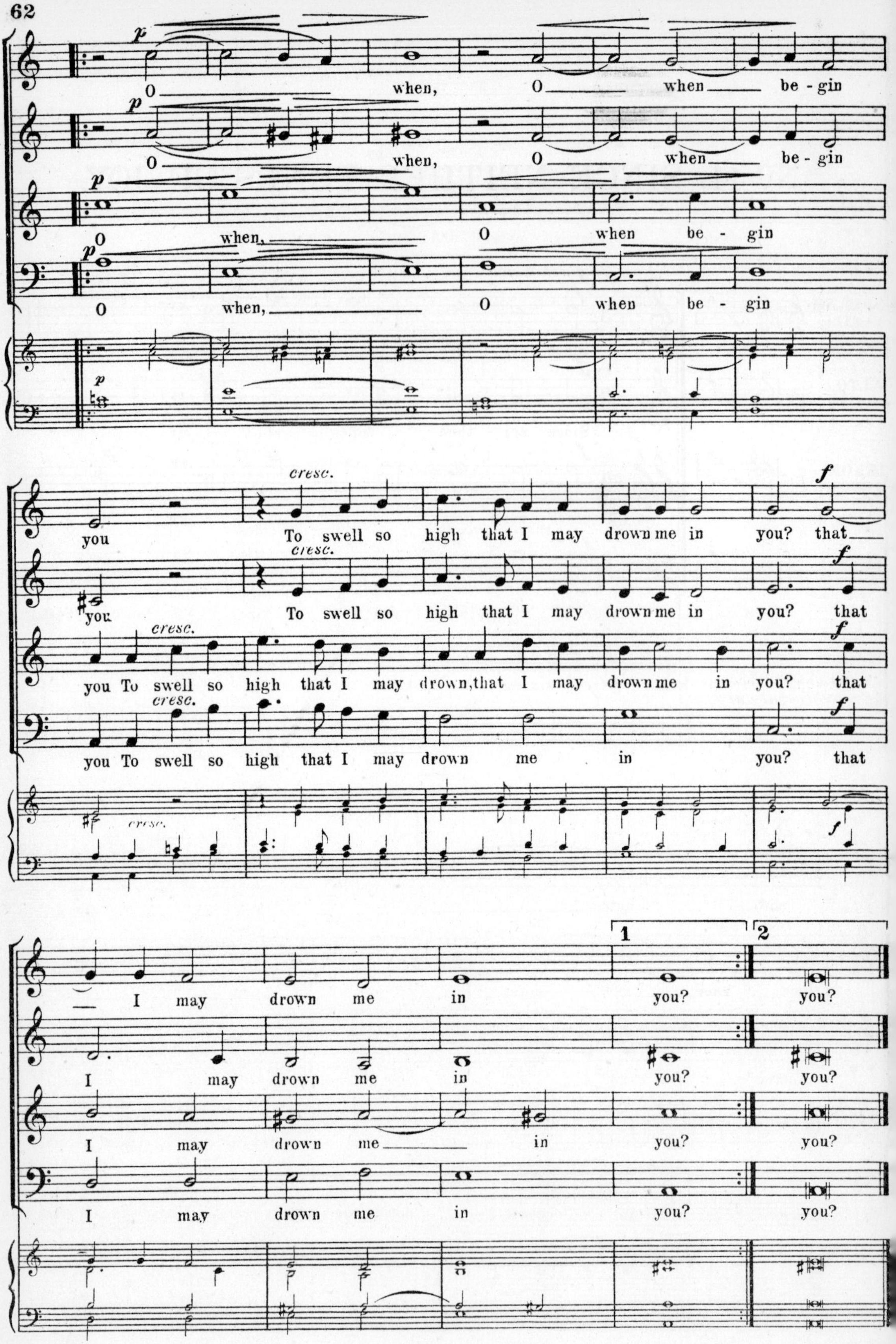
p
O when, O when be-gin
p
O when, O when be-gin
p
O when, O when be-gin
p
O when, O when be-gin
p
cresc.
you To swell so high that I may drown me in you? that
cresc.
you To swell so high that I may drown me in you? that
cresc.
you To swell so high that I may drown, that I may drown me in you? that
cresc.
you To swell so high that I may drown me in you? that
cresc.
f
I may drown me in you? you?
I may drown me in you? you?
I may drown me in you? you?
I may drown me in you? you?
1
2

Nº 14. SINCE NEITHER TUNES OF JOY.

cresc.
Cru - el un - kind, can move thee, I will go run a - way, I
Cru - el un - kind, can move thee, I will go
Cru - el un - kind, can move thee, I will go run a way, I
Cru - el un - kind, can move thee,
f
will go run a - way for rage and mad - ness, for
run a - way, I will go run a - way for rage, for rage
will go run a - way, I will go run, I will go run a - way for
I will go run a - way, I will go run a - way for
rage and mad - ness, Be - cause I will not love thee. O
and mad - ness, Be - cause I will not love thee. O come
rage and mad - ness, Be - cause I will not love thee. O
rage and mad - ness, Be - cause I will not love thee. O
p

come a - gain, a - gain, O come a - gain, a - gain,
a - gain, a - gain, O come a - gain, a - gain,
come a - gain, a - gain, O come a - gain, a - gain,
come a - gain, a - gain, O come a - gain, a - gain,
thy fruit - less la - bour waste not,
thy fruit - less la - bour waste not, How wilt thou run
thy fruit - less la - bour waste not, How wilt thou run
thy fruit - less la - bour waste not, How wilt thou
f
How wilt thou run
fool, how wilt thou
fool, how wilt thou run
run fool,

mf
fool, how wilt thou run fool, when thy
run how wilt thou run fool, when thy
fool, when thy
how wilt thou run fool, when thy
p
heart thou hast not, when thy heart thou hast
f
1.
2.
not, when thy heart thou hast not? O not?
not, when thy heart thou hast not? O come not?
not, when thy heart thou hast not? O not?

No. 15. O GRIEF! WHERE SHALL POOR GRIEF?

mf
— find pa - tient hear - ing? Foot - steps of men I fly, foot -
mf
hear - ing, find pa - tient hear - ing? Foot -
mf
— find pa - tient hear - ing? Foot-steps of men I — fly, I
mf
Foot - steps of men I fly, — I
mf
- steps of men I fly, — I fly,
- steps of men I fly, — I
fly, foot - steps of men I —
fly, I fly, — foot - steps of men I —
p
I fly, I fly, — my paths each crea - ture
p
fly, I — fly, my paths each crea - ture
p
fly, I — fly, — my paths each crea - ture
p
fly, I fly, I fly, my paths each crea - ture
p

baulk - ing: Wild and un - haunt - ed woods,
baulk - ing: Wild and un - haunt - ed woods, un - haunt -
baulk - ing: Wild and un - haunt - ed woods, wild and un -
baulk - ing: Wild and un - haunt - ed
— wild and un - haunt - ed woods seem
- ed woods, wild and un - haunt - ed
-haunt - ed woods, wild and un - haunt -
woods, seem tir -
tir - ed with my walk -
woods seem tir - ed with my
- ed woods seem tir - ed
- ed with my walk - ing,

p
ing. Earth with my
p>
walk - ing. Earth with my tears
p
with my walk - ing. Earth with my tears are
p
Earth with my tears are
p
mf
tears are drunk: Air with my sighs tor -
mf
are drunk: Air with my sighs tor -
mf
drunk: Air with my sighs tor - ment
mf
drunk: Air with my sighs tor - ment
mf
f
ment - ed: Heav - ens
f
ment - ed: Heav - ens with my
f
ed: Heav - ens with my cry -
f
ed: Heav - ens with my
f

with my cry - ing, heav - ens with my cry -
cry - ing, heav - ens with my cry - ing grown
-ing, heav - ens with my cry - - ing,
cry - ing, heav - ens with my cry - ing,
- - ing, grown deaf, grown deaf,
deaf with my cry - ing grown deaf,
with my cry - ing grown deaf,
with my cry - ing grown deaf,
and dis - con - tent - ed, and
and dis - con - tent - -
and dis - con - tent - ed, and
and dis - con - tent - - ed,

* No fresh time signature is printed in any of the parts in these two places but the great length of the notes seem to suggest that $\frac{3}{1}$ was intended for these two bars.

love loves my la-ment-ing, loves my la-ment-ing, on-ly my love
my la-ment-ing, loves my la-ment-ing, on-ly my love loves
my la-ment-ing, loves my la-ment ing, on-ly my love loves my
my la-ment-ing, loves my la-ment-ing, on-ly my love
loves my la-ment-ing.
my la-ment-ing, la-ment-ing.
la-ment-ing, la-ment-ing.
loves my la-ment-ing.

Nº 16. O SWEET GRIEF.

-ing: O sweet re - puls - es, O
-ing: O sweet re - puls - es, O sweet re - puls -
-ing: O sweet re - puls - es, O sweet re -
-ing: O sweet re - puls - es, O sweet re -
sweet re - puls - es, sweet wrongs, sweet wrongs,
-es, sweet wrongs, sweet wrongs, sweet la - ment -
-puls - es, sweet wrongs, sweet la - ment -
-puls - es, sweet wrongs, sweet wrongs, sweet la -
sweet la - ment - ing. Words
- - ing, sweet la - ment - ing. Words sharp - ly
-ing, sweet la - ment - ing. Words sharp - ly sweet,
-ment - - ing, sweet la - ment - ing. Words sharp - ly

sharp - ly sweet, sharp - ly sweet and
sweet and sweet - ly sharp con - sent - ing, con -
sharp - ly sweet and sweet - ly sharp, sweet - ly sharp con -
sweet, words sharp - ly sweet and sweet - ly
sweet - ly sharp con - sent - ing, and sweet -
- sent - ing, and sweet - ly
- sent - ing, con - sent - ing, words sweet -
sharp con - sent - ing, con - sent - ing, and
- ly sharp con - sent - ing, O
sharp con - sent - ing, O sweet
- ly sharp con - sent - ing, O
sweet - ly sharp con - sent - ing, O sweet
p
p
p
p
p

sweet un - kind - ness, sweet fears, sweet com -
un kind ness, sweet fears, sweet com -
sweet un - kind - ness, sweet fears,
un - kind - ness, sweet fears, sweet com -
mf
-plain - ing. Grieve then no more, my soul, those
- plain - ing. Grieve then no more, my soul,
sweet com-plain - ing. Grieve then no more, my soul, those
-plain - - ing. Grieve then no more, my soul, those
deep groans strain - - ing,
those deep groans strain - ing, Your bit-ter an-guish now shall
deep groans strain - ing, Your bit-ter an - guish now shall
deep groans strain - ing, Your bit-ter an - guish now
f

* This note is printed F in the original edition.

Nº 17. REST NOW, AMPHION.

- - on, rest, rest rest thy charm-ing lyre, thy
-phi - on, rest, rest rest thy charm - ing
- - on, rest, rest thy charm-ing lyre,
- - on, rest, rest thy charm - ing lyre,
charm-ing lyre, thy charm-ing lyre,
lyre, thy charm-ing lyre, thy charm-ing lyre, For Daph -
thy charm-ing lyre, For Daph - ne's
thy charm-ing lyre, For Daph -
mf
For Daph - ne's love, sweet love, makes me -
-ne's love, sweet love, makes me - lo - dy, sweet love makes me - lo -
love, sweet love, for Daph - ne's love makes
-ne's love, sweet love makes me - lo - dy, for Daph - ne's

- lo - dy, makes me - lo - dy, for Daph -
-dy, for Daph - ne's love, sweet love, makes me - lo -
me - lo - dy, for Daph - ne's love, for
love, for Daph-ne's love makes me-lo - dy, for Daph-ne's love, sweet
- ne's love, makes me - lo - dy, Her
-dy, makes me - lo - dy, Her
Daph-ne's love, sweet love makes me - lo - dy, me - lo -
love makes mel - o - dy, makes me - lo - dy,
love's con - cord with mine doth well con - spire, doth well
love's con - cord with mine doth well con - spire,
-dy, Her love's con - cord with
Her

— con - spire, her love's con - cord with mine doth
— doth well con - - - spire,
mine doth well con - spire, No dis - cord
love's con - cord with mine doth well con - spire, No dis -
well con - spire, No dis - cord jars, no
No dis - cord jars in our loves'
jars in our loves' sym - pa - thy, no
- cord jars in our loves' sym - pa - -
dis - cord jars, no dis - cord jars in our loves'
sym - pa - thy, no dis - cord jars in our loves'
— dis - cord jars, no dis - cord jars in our loves'
- thy, no dis - cord jars in our love's sym - pa -

sym - pa - thy, Our con-cords have some dis - cords
sym - pa - thy, Our con-cords have some dis -
sym - pa - thy, Our con-cords have some
-thy, Our con - cords have some dis - cords
mixed a - mong, Dis - cord - ing
- cords mixed a - mong, Dis - cord -
dis - cords mixed a - mong, Dis - cord - ing con -
mixed a - mong,
con - cords makes the sweet - est song,
- ing con - cords makes the sweet - est song,
- cords makes the sweet - est song, dis - cord -
Dis - cord - ing con - - -
p
mf

dis - cord - ing con - cords makes the sweet - est
makes the sweet - est song,
- ing con - cords makes the sweet - est song, dis -
-cords dis - - cord - ing
song, dis - cord - ing con - cords, dis -
dis - cord - ing con -
- cord - ing con - cords, dis - cord -
con - cords makes the sweet - est, sweet - est
- cord - ing con - cords makes the sweet - est song.
-cords, con - cords makes the sweet - est song.
- ing con - cords makes the sweet - est song.
song, makes the sweet - est song.

A Madrigal by John Bennet

included by Thomas Morley as Nº 4. in
"THE TRIUMPHS OF ORIANA."
(1601)

Edited by EDMUND H. FELLOWES.

ALL CREATURES NOW.

p
mer - ry - mind - ed, The shep-herds' daugh-ters play - ing, the
mer - ry - mind - ed, The shep - herds' daugh-ters
p
mind - - - ed, The shep-herds' daugh-ters play - ing, the
mer - ry - mind - ed, The shep - herds' daugh-ters
p
- - - ed, The shep-herds' daugh-ters play - ing, the
p
f
shep - herds' daugh - ters play - ing, The
p
play - ing, the shep - herds' daugh - ters play - ing,
f
shep - herds' daugh - ters play - ing, are play - ing, are play - ing, The
p
play - ing, the shep - herds' daugh - ters play - ing,
f
shep - herds' daugh - ters play - ing, The
f

Nymphs are Fa - la - la - ing, the Nymphs are Fa - la - la - ing,
The Nymphs are Fa - la - la - ing, the Nymphs are Fa - la -
Nymphs are Fa - la - la - ing, the Nymphs are Fa - la - la - ing Fa - la - la - la -
The Nymphs are Fa - la - la - ing, the Nymphs are Fa - la -
Nymphs are Fa - la - la - ing, the Nymphs are Fa - la - la - ing

the Nymphs are Fa - la - la - la - la - ing. Yond bu - gle was well
-la - ing, the Nymphs are Fa - la - la - ing. Yond bu - gle was well
-la - ing, Fa - la - la - la - la - la - la - ing. Yond bu - gle was well
-la - ing, the Nymphs are Fa - la - la - la - la - la - ing. Yond bu - gle was well
the Nymph are Fa - la - la - la - la - ing. Yond bu - gle was well

wind - - ed. At O - ri - a - naes pres - ence each thing
wind - - ed. At O - ri a - naes pres - ence each thing
wind - ed. At O - ri - a - naes pres - ence each thing—
wind - - ed. At O - ri - a - naes pres - ence each thing
wind - - ed. At O - ri - a - naes pres - ence each thing
p
smil - eth, The flowers them-selves dis - cov - er, the flowers them-selves dis -
smil - eth, The flowers them-selves dis - cov - er, the flowers them-selves dis -
— smil - eth, The flowers them-selves dis - cov - er, the flowers them - selves
smil - eth, The flowers them - selves dis - cov - er, the flowers them-selves dis -
smil - eth, The flowers them-selves dis - cov - er, the flowers them-selves dis -

-cov - er, Birds o-ver her do ho - - ver,
- cov - er, Birds o-ver her do ho - - ver,
dis-cov - er, Birds o-ver her do ho - - ver,
-cov - - er, Birds o-ver her do ho - - ver,
-cov - er, Birds o-ver her do ho - ver,

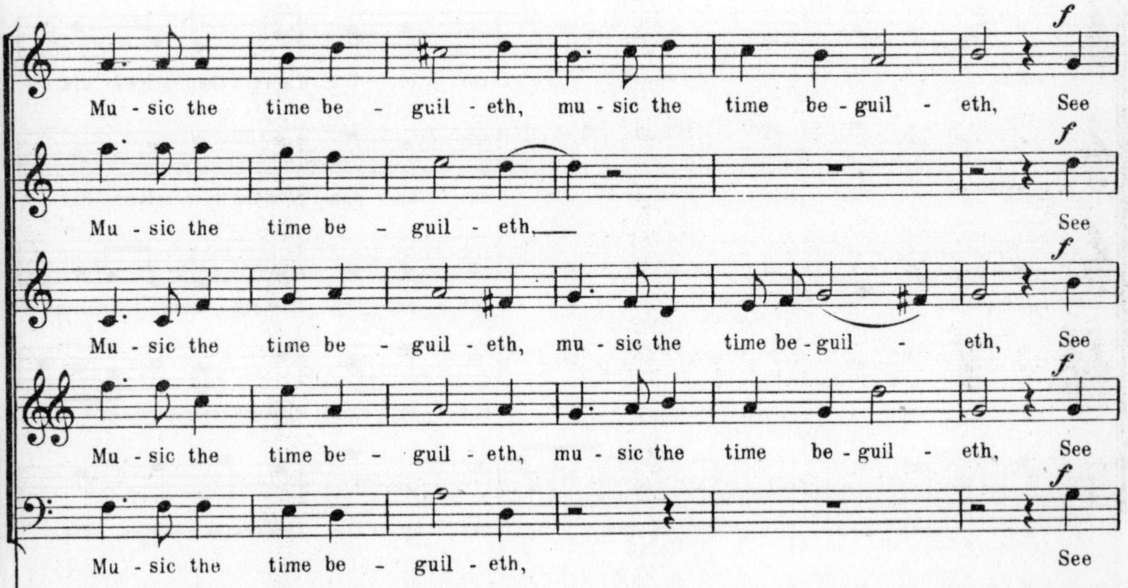
f
Mu-sic the time be - guil - eth, mu-sic the time be-guil - eth, See
f
Mu-sic the time be - guil - eth,
See
f
Mu-sic the time be - guil - eth, mu-sic the time be-guil - eth, See
f
Mu-sic the time be - guil - eth, mu-sic the time be-guil - eth, See
f
Mu-sic the time be - guil - eth,
See
f

where she comes, see where she comes with flower - y gar - lands crown - ed, Queen
where she comes, see where she comes with flower - y gar - lands crown - ed, Queen of all
where she comes, see where she comes with flower - y gar - lands crown - ed, Queen of all
where she comes, see where she comes with flower - y gar - lands crown - ed,
where she comes, see where she comes with flower - y gar - lands crown - ed, Queen of all
of all queens re - nown - ed, Queen of all queens re - nown - ed.
queens re - nown - ed, Queen of all queens re - - nown - ed.
queens re - nown - ed, Queen of all queens re - nown - ed.
Queen of all queens re - nown - ed, re - nown - ed.
queens re - nown - ed, Queen of all queens re - nown - ed.

mf
Then sang the shep-herds and Nymphs of Di - a - na, Nymphs of Di -
Then sang the shep-herds and Nymphs of Di - a - na, Nymphs of Di -
Then sang the shep-herds and Nymphs of Di - a - na, Nymphs of Di -
Then sang the shep-herds and Nymphs of Di - a - na, Nymphs of Di -
Then sang the shep-herds and Nymphs of Di - a - na, Nymphs of Di -
f
-a - na, Long live fair
-a - na, Long live fair O - - ri -
-a - na, Long live fair O - ri - a - na,
-a - na, Long live fair O - ri - a -
-a - na, Long live fair O - ri - a - -

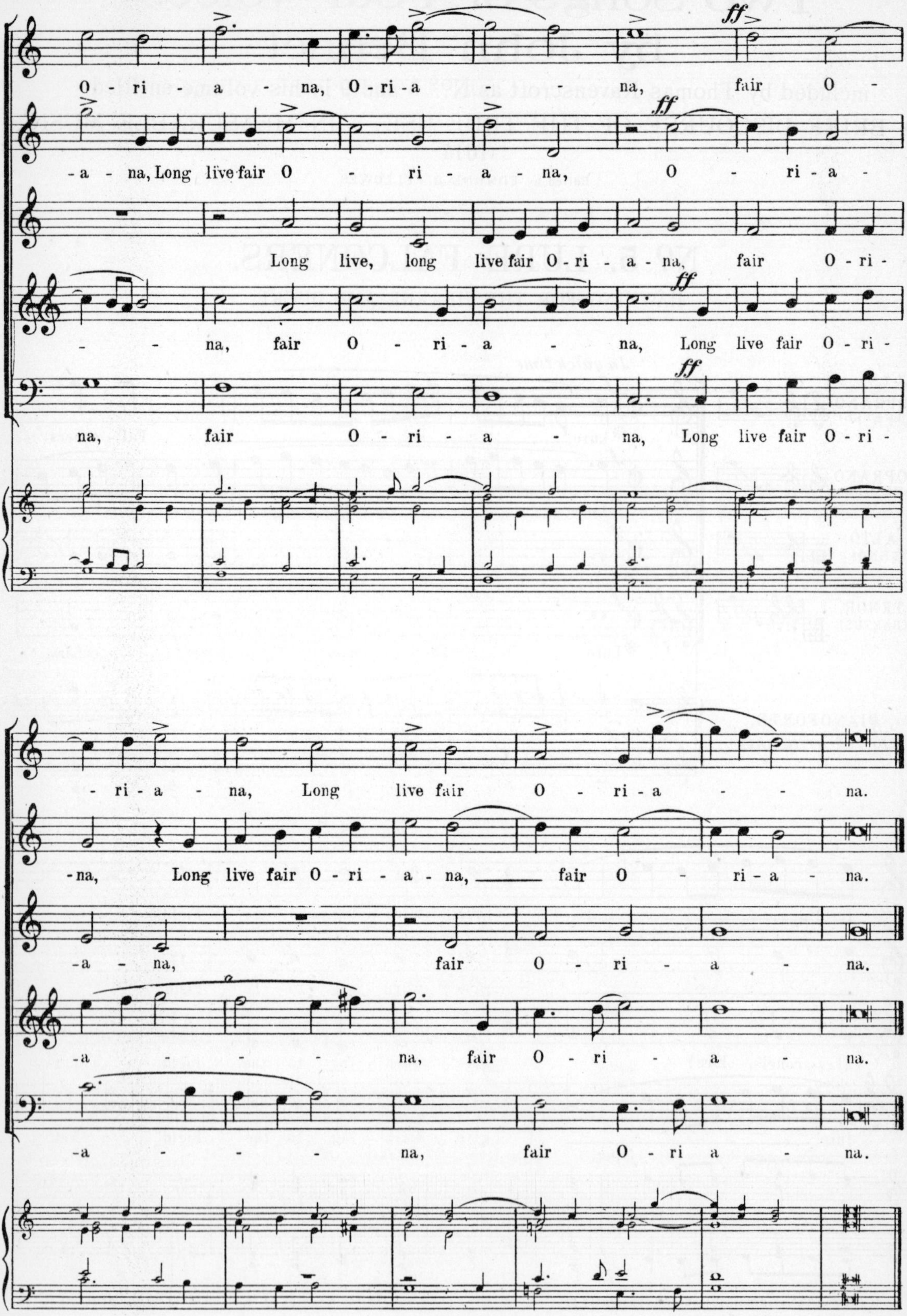
O - ri - a - na, O - ri - a - na, fair O -
-a - na, Long live fair O - ri - a - na, O - ri - a -
Long live, long live fair O - ri - a - na, fair O - ri -
- - na, fair O - ri - a - na, Long live fair O - ri -
na, fair O - ri - a - na, Long live fair O - ri -
ff
- ri - a - na, Long live fair O - ri - a - na.
-na, Long live fair O - ri - a - na, fair O - ri - a - na.
-a - na, fair O - ri - a - na.
-a - na, fair O - ri - a - na.
-a - na, fair O - ri a - na.

Two Songs of Four Voices by John Bennet

included by Thomas Ravenscroft as Nos. 5 and 9 in his volume entitled

A BRIEF DISCOURSE OF THE TRUE USE. . . IN MEASURABLE MUSIC.

(1614)

Edited by EDMUND H FELLOWES

No 5. LURE FALCONERS.

HAWKING FOR THE HEARNE AND DUCKE.

*Spelt *luer* in the original edition, and apparently pronounced in two syllables: For the meaning of this and other technical terms in this song see Notes on page IX.

†Two quavers are missing in the original edition in the Tenor part.

§These two notes are printed as quavers in the original edition.

Let fly, let fly! make mount-ing Hearnes to yield, make
Let fly, let fly! make mount-ing Hearnes to yield, make
fly, let fly, let fly! make mount-ing Hearnes to yield, make
fly, let fly, let fly! make mount-ing Hearnes to yield, make
mount - ing Hearnes to yield, Die, fear - ful Ducks, and
mount - ing Hearnes to yield, Die, fear - ful Ducks, and
mount - ing Hearnes to yield, Die, fear - ful Ducks, die
mount - ing Hearnes to yield, Die, fear - ful Ducks, and
p
climb no more so high, and climb no more so high, and
climb no more so high, no more so high, and climb no
fear - ful Ducks, and climb no more so high, and climb no
climb no more so high, and climb no more so high, no more so

*This variant occurs in the Tenor part in the original edition.
†This variant occurs in the Bassus part of the original edition.

lo, hey lo, hey lo! Hey lo, hey lo, hey lo,
lo, hey lo, hey lo! Hey lo, hey lo, hey lo!
lo! Hey lo, hey lo, hey lo, hey lo, hey lo!
lo, hey lo hey lo! Hey lo, hey
1.
2.
p
hey lo, hey lo! But lo!
Hey lo, hey lo, hey lo, hey lo! But lo!
Hey lo, hey lo, hey lo! But lo!
lo! Hey lo, hey lo! But lo!

Nº 9. ROUND ABOUT IN A FAIR RING.

THE ELVES DANCE.

In quick time.*
SOPRANO. (TREBLE.)
Round a-bout, round a-bout in a fair ring a,
SOPRANO. (MEDIUS.)
Round a-bout, round a-bout in a fair ring a,
ALTO. (TENOR.)
Round a-bout, round a-bout in a fair ring a,
TENOR. (BASSUS.)
Round a-bout, round a-bout in a fair ring a,
PIANOFORTE. (For rehearsal only.)

Thus we dance, thus we dance, and thus we sing a,
Thus we dance, thus we dance, and thus we sing a,
Thus we dance, thus we dance, and thus we sing a,
Thus we dance, thus we dance, and thus we sing a,

*The minim must be treated as having the crotchet value throughout this song.

mf
Trip and trip and go, to and fro, and fro, to and fro,
mf
Trip and trip and go, to and fro, and fro, to
mf
Trip and trip and go, to and fro, and
mf
Trip and trip and go, to and fro, and fro, to and
mf
to and fro, o - ver this green a,
— and to and fro, o - ver this green a,
fro, and fro, o - ver this green a,
to and fro, and fro, o - ver this green a,

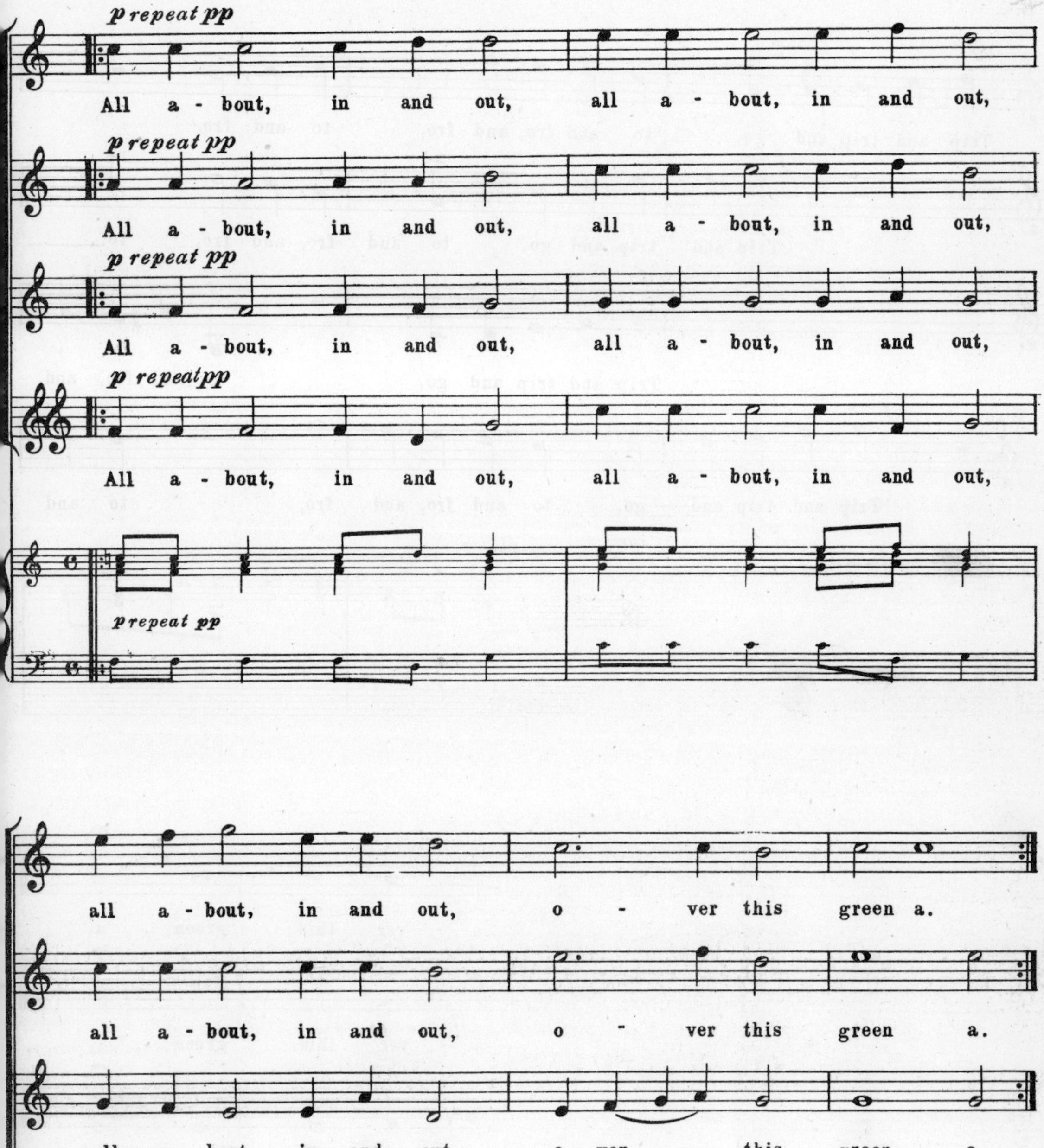

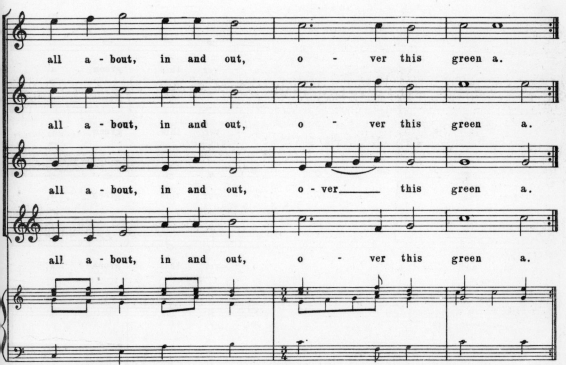

Lowe and Brydone (Printers) Limited, London

INDEX

THE ENGLISH MADRIGALISTS

Edited by
EDMUND H. FELLOWES

Revised by Thurston Dart

24

GEORGE KIRBYE

FIRST SET OF MADRIGALS (1597)

Associate Reviser for this Volume: Philip Brett

STAINER & BELL, LTD.,
29 NEWMAN STREET, LONDON, W.1

AMERICAN AGENTS:
GALAXY MUSIC CORPORATION, NEW YORK

MADE IN GREAT BRITAIN

NOTE

The musical and verbal texts have been checked (and, where necessary, corrected) from the British Museum Royal Music set of the original part-books. Further details of Kirbye's life will be found in the current edition of Grove's *Dictionary*, with a bibliographical note by G. E. P. Arkwright.

Jesus College,
Cambridge,
Spring, 1960.

THURSTON DART

PREFACE TO VOL. XXIV.

IT has not been thought necessary to reprint in each volume of this Series the full explanation of the methods adopted by the Editor, especially as the Preface to Volume I. is published separately, and can be obtained separately by those who have not a copy of that volume. It is very important, however, to emphasize that a thorough grasp of the principles which are explained in detail in that treatise is absolutely indispensable for a clear understanding and practical use of this Edition, and particular attention is directed to the paragraph on Rhythm and Barring.

The musical illustrations there employed are drawn exclusively from the works of Thomas Morley, but the principles which they illustrate apply to the whole of this Series.

The following points are fully dealt with under separate headings:—

1. Clefs.
2. Words.
3. Expression.
4. Rhythm and Barring.
5. Repeat Marks.
6. Time-signatures.
7. Key-signatures.
8. Accidentals.
9. Pianoforte Score.

Though I have used every endeavour to reproduce an accurate version of the original text throughout this Series, I am aware that in a work of this magnitude it is almost inevitable that some misprints should escape detection in reading the proofs. I shall be glad to have any such misprints brought to my notice, so that they may be corrected in future editions. I shall also welcome any information as to the authorship of any of the lyrics not hitherto identified.

Our knowledge of the details of Kirbye's life, such as they are, is due almost entirely to the researches of Mr. Godfrey Arkwright.

It is probable that the date of his birth was about 1565; but the details are wanting, and his birthplace is also unknown. He was a contributor to East's "The Whole Book of Psalms" in 1592. He held the position of household musician in the service of Sir Robert Jermyn at Rushbrooke Hall in Suffolk, where he was a near neighbour of John Wilbye at Hengrave. In the latter years of his life he lived in Whiting Street, Bury St. Edmunds, where he owned a house. He took an interest in parochial affairs at that period and was at one time Churchwarden of St. Mary's, Bury St. Edmunds. He died in 1634, and both he and his wife, whose death took place in 1626, were buried at St. Mary's Church. His will, which Mr. Arkwright has printed in full in his Old English Edition (Part 5), was proved at Bury.

Kirbye at one time enjoyed a considerable reputation as a madrigalist, but in latter days his memory, as well as his work, had been unduly neglected until Mr. Arkwright did so much to revive it. He was praised by Dr. Burney in his history as one of the best of the English madrigalists. Kirbye's work is not perhaps quite in the highest rank of the English madrigal school, yet much of it is attractive; and as a whole this Set is well up to the high standard which has made this band of English musicians so famous.

Besides the set of madrigals published in 1597, this volume contains Kirbye's contribution to the "Triumphs of Oriana." There appear to have been two editions of that collection published in 1601; and although the music is precisely the same, the words of Kirbye's madrigal are entirely different in the two editions. In what is apparently the first edition the words of the poem set by Kirbye begin "Bright Phœbus greets most clearly," but in the second edition there is substituted a poem beginning "With angel's face and brightness," a poem set by Norcome for the "Triumphs." There is not a shadow of doubt on internal evidence that these latter words were those set by Kirbye in the first place, and it must be supposed that the alternative version was substituted either by Morley or by East, the printer, who seems to have had a very free hand in these matters, if we may judge from his dealings with Bateson, for example. They may have wished to avoid the repetition of Norcome's words. It may be conjectured that Kirbye resented the substitution of other words, which certainly much marred the subtler points of his madrigal, and that the original words were replaced as a result of his protest.

EDMUND H. FELLOWES.

THE CLOISTERS,
WINDSOR CASTLE.
September 1st, 1918.

LYRICS

SET TO MUSIC BY

GEORGE KIRBYE

In his Madrigals to 4, 5 & 6 voices.

I.

Lo, here I leave my heart with her remaining,
That never yet did deign to do me pleasure.
And when I seek to move her with complaining,
She scorns my sighs and tears, alas, past measure.
Sweet Love, O turn her heart at last and joy me,
Or else her deep disdain will soon destroy me.

II.

Alas, what hope of speeding
Where Hope beguiled lies bleeding ?
She bade come when she spied me,
And when I came she flied me.
Then when I was beguiled
She at my sighing smiled.
But if you take such pleasure
Of hope and joy, my treasure,
By deceit to bereave me,
Love me, and so deceive me.

III.

What can I do, my dearest, of the sweet help deprived
Of those thy fair eyes, by which I still have lived ?
How can my soul endure, thus charged with sadness;
Exile from thy dear sight, so full of gladness ?

IV.

Woe am I ! when my heart dies,
As that which on thy will relies.
Since, then, I die only in hope to please thee
No grief of death, though cruel, shall disease me.
Yet shall I be tormented,
Cruel, to see thee pleased and contented.

V.

Farewell, my love, I part contented
Since 'tis ordained that I must leave thee.
O might I stay, although tormented!
The pain next death would little grieve me.
No greater torment can be proved
Than thus to part from my beloved.

VI.

Sleep now, my Muse, and henceforth take thy rest,
Which all too long thyself in vain had wasted.
Let it suffice I still must live oppressed,
And of my pains the fruit must ne'er be tasted.
Then sleep, my Muse, Fate cannot be withstood;
'Tis better sleep, than wake and do no good.

VII.

Ah, sweet, alas, when first I saw those eyes,
Those eyes so rich with crystal majesty,
Their wounding beauty 'gan to tyrannize
And made mine eyes bleed tears full piteously.
I felt the wound, yet feared I not the deed
Till, ah, I found my tears did inward bleed.

VIII.

Mourn now, my soul, with anguish of my pains;
Crossed are my joys which hope did ever give;
Dry are mine eyes with shedding tears in vain;
Dead is my heart which never more can live;
Hard are my torments, living thus in grief,
Harder her heart that yieldeth no relief.

IX.

(*The first part.*)

Sound out, my voice, with pleasant tunes recording
The new delight that love to me inspireth,
Pleased and content with that my mind desireth.
Thanked be love, so heavenly joys affording.

X.

(*The second part.*)

She, that my plaints with rigour long rejected,
Binding my heart with those her golden tresses
In recompense of all my long distresses
Said with a sigh: Thy love hath me infected.

XI.

What? Shall I part thus unregarded
From you, whom death could not dissever?
Is faithful service thus rewarded?
Why, then, vain hope, adieu for ever!

XII.

(*The first part.*)

Sorrow consumes me, and instead of rest
With folded arms I sadly sit and weep;
And if I wink it is for fear to see
The fearful dreams' effects that trouble me.

XIII.

(*The second part.*)

O heavens, what shall I do? Alas, must I,
Must I myself be murderer of myself?
Must I myself be forced to ope the way
Whereat my soul in wounds may sally forth?
Hard is my hap! and thus in grief I die.

XIV.

Why should I love since she doth prove ungrateful,
Since for reward I reap nought but disdain?
Love thus to be requited it is hateful,
And Reason would I should not love in vain.
Yet all in vain when all is out of season,
For Love hath no society with Reason.

XV.

Sweet love, O cease thy flying
And pity me now dying.
To ease my heart distressed
With haste make thy returning
And quench my restless burning,
That I by you redressed
May be revived and honour you as blessed.

XVI.

That Muse which sung the beauty of thy face
In sweet well-tuned songs
And harmony that pleased,
If still I be diseased,
Can carol of thy wrongs,
And blaze these faults that will thy worth disgrace.
Yet if thou dost repent thee
I will forgive, that mends shall well content thee.

XVII.

See what a maze of error
And labyrinth of terror
My love hath traced.
I, wretched, whom love paineth
And true love only gaineth,
Hope utterly disgraced
And by disdain defaced.

XVIII.

If Pity reign with Beauty,
Then may I be assured
That what my harm procured
Will yield me help of duty;
For wrongful was she never.
Then why should I still in despair persever?

XIX.

Ah, cruel hateful fortune!
Now must I death importune.
Since that I am of all my hope deprived,
Nor but for sorrow hath my soul survived.
Only this hope doth rest for my contentment—
That fortune tired will yield me some amendment.

XX.

I love, alas, yet am I not beloved.
My suits are all rejected
And all my looks suspected.
Experience now too late hath proved
That 'twas in vain that erst I loved.

XXI.

O must I part, my jewel,
Hapless from my fair sun whose beams me nourish?
Who now comforteth, or doth me cherish
Pained, alas, with grief so cruel?
O if it so must needs be,
How can my wicked fortune further harm me?

XXII.

(*The first part.*)

Up, then, Melpomene! the mournful'st Muse of nine,
Such cause of mourning never hadst afore.
Up, grisly ghosts! and up, my rueful rhyme!
Matter of mirth now shalt thou have no more,
For dead she is that mirth thee made of yore.
Dido my dear, alas, is dead,
Dead and lieth wrapped in lead.
O heavy hearse!
Let streaming tears be poured out in store.
O careful verse!

Edmund Spenser.

XXIII.

(*The second part.*)

Why wail we thus? why weary we the gods with plaints
As if some evil were to her betight?
She reigns, a goddess now among the saints
That whilom was the saint of shepherds' light
And is installed now in heaven's height.
I see thee, blessed soul, I see
Walk in Elysian fields so free.
O happy hearse!
Might I once come to thee! O that I might!
O joyful verse!

Edmund Spenser.

XXIV.

The words are the same as those of No. VI.

From "THE TRIUMPHS OF ORIANA."

With angel's face and brightness
And Orient hue fair Oriana shining,
With nimble foot she tripped o'er hills and mountains
Hard by Diana's fountains.
At last in dale she rested.
This is that maiden Queen of fairyland
With sceptre in her hand.
The Fauns and Satyrs dancing
Did show their nimble lightness.
Fair Nais and the nymphs did leave their bowers
And brought their baskets full of herbs and flowers.
Then sang the shepherds and nymphs of Diana:
Long live fair Oriana!

(*Alternative version of words to this madrigal.*)

Bright Phœbus greets most clearly
With radiant beams fair Oriana sitting.
Her apple Venus yields as best befitting
A Queen beloved most dearly.
And Proserpine glad runs in her best array:
Nymphs deck her crown with bay.
Her feet are lions kissing.
No joy can there be missing.
Now Thetis leaves the mermaids' tunes admired
And swells with pride to see this Queen desired.
Then sang the shepherds and nymphs of Diana:
Long live fair Oriana!

NOTES

XVI.—Line 4. *diseased.* Used in the old sense of being *ill at ease.*

Line 8. *mends—reparation.*

XXII. & XXIII.—This pcem is from the "November" ecologue of Edmund Spenser's "Shepherd's Calendar."

The alternative words to Kirbye's Oriana madrigal appear in the two editions of "The Triumphs," both of which were published in 1601. There can be no doubt at all that Kirbye set his music firstly to the words of *With angel's face and brightness.* (See Preface to the present volume.)

The firſt ſet

OF ENGLISH

Madrigalls,

to 4. 5. & 6. voyces.

Made and newly publiſhed

by

George Kirbye.

LONDON
Printed by Thomas Eſte
dwelling in alderſgate
ſtreet

1597.

To the vertuous, and very worthy Gentlewo-

men, Miſtris Anne : & Miſtris Frauncis Iermin,

daughters to the right worſhipfull, Syr Robert Iermin

Knight, (his very good Maiſter) G.K. wiſheth

in this life, increaſe of all vertues, and in

the life to come, the full fruition

of all happineſſe.

IT were a thing very vnneceſſary (thriſe worthy & vertuous gentlewomen) for mee (although I were able) to ſpeake any thing in commendation & praiſe of Muſicke, conſidering (beſides that many learned men haue learnedly written in commendation thereof) the examples of times paſt, and our owne experience euery day, doth giue sufficient teſtimonie both of the pleaſure & proffit that it bringeth to a diſtreſſed & melancholy mind. Alſo I think it conuenient not to anſwere (otherwiſe then with ſilence) to thoſe (more ſenceleſſe then brute beaſtes) that with open mouthes doe in-veigh, & ſpeake all the euill they can againſt that excellent knowledge. But it ſtandeth mee in hand, rather to craue pardon, for this my boldnes, in putting to the veiw of ſo many learned Muſitions, (which this age & Realme affordeth) theſe firſt fruites of my poor knowledge in Muſicke, yet I hope, that as they them ſelues had ſmall entrances, beefore they came to their perfection, ſo they will fauourably, accept of theſe beginnings, looking for better hereafter : And in hope of their better likings, I haue made choiſe of you to patroniſe theſe my labours, as well for the Haereditarie vertues of your godly parentes alreadie dwelling in you, as alſo for the delight, knowledge, & practiſe which you haue in Muſicke, in the which few or none (that I know) can excell you. Vouchſafe therefore (worthy Miſtriſſes) to vndertake the tuition of that, which by right & equitie, you may challenge for your owne, being no ſtraungers, but home bredd, & which for your delight & cōtentments were firſt by me compiled : & as you ſeemed to like them, being mine, ſo I doe not doubt but you will more fauour them, now beeing your owne. Then I (your deuoted ſeruant) ſhall think my paines heerein very well rewarded, & be better encouraged to employ my time hereafter in your further ſeruice.

Yours in all duetie,

George Kirbye.

TABLE OF CONTENTS

George Kirbye's Madrigals

TO

Four, Five, and Six Voices.

(1597)

Edited by EDMUND H. FELLOWES.

Revised by Thurston Dart.

No. 1. LO HERE MY HEART I LEAVE.

Lo here my heart I leave with her re - main - - ing, that
here my heart I leave with her re - main - ing, that
heart I leave, I leave with her re - main - ing, that
Lo here my heart I leave with her re - main - - ing, that
nev - er yet did deign to do me plea - sure, and when I seek to move her
nev - er yet did deign to do me plea - sure,
nev - er yet did deign to do me plea - sure, and when I seek to move her with
nev - er yet did deign to do me plea - sure, and when I seek to move her
with com - plain - ing, com - plain - ing, and when I seek to
and when I seek to move her with com - plain - ing,
com - plain - ing, and when I seek to move her
with com - plain - ing, and when I seek to

move her with com - plain - ing,
com - plain - ing, she scorns my sighs and tears a -
with com - plain - ing, com - plain - ing, she scorns my sighs and tears
move her with com - plain - ing, she scorns my
she scorns my sighs and tears a - las past mea - sure, she scorns my
- las past mea - sure, a - las past mea - sure she scorns my
past mea - sure, she scorns my sighs and tears a - las past mea -
sighs and tears a - las past mea - sure, she
sighs and tears a - las past mea - sure. sweet
sighs and tears a - las past mea - sure. sweet
- sure, a - las past mea sure. sweet
scorns my sighs and tears a - las past mea - sure. sweet
p
f

*In this repeat the Cantus Primus and Secundus interchange parts.

Nº 2. ALAS, WHAT HOPE OF SPEEDING?

mf
p
what hope of speed - ing where hope be-guiled lies bleed -
mf
p
- las, what hope of speed - ing where hope be-guiled lies bleed -
mf
p
- las, what hope of speed - ing where hope be-guiled lies bleed -
mf
p
- las, what hope of speed - ing where hope be-guiled lies bleed -
mf
p
- ing? she bade come when she
mf
- ing? she bade come when she
mf
- ing? she bade come when she spied me, she bade come when she
mf
- ing? she bade come when she spied me, when she
mf
spied me, and when I came, she flied me,
p
spied me. and when I came, she flied me,
p
spied me, and when I came, she flied me,
p
spied me,
p

mf
and when I came, she flied
and when I came, she flied me.
and when I came, she flied
and when I came, she flied
p
me. thus when I was be-guil-ed, thus when I was be-
thus when I was be-guil-ed, be-guil-ed, be-
me. thus when I was be-guil-ed, be-
thus when I was be-
mf
-guil-ed, she at my sigh-ing smil-
-guil-ed, she at my sigh-ing smil-
-guil-ed, she at my sigh-ing, she at my sigh-ing
-guil-ed,

- - ed, she at my sigh - ing, she at my sigh - ing
- - ed, she at my sigh - ing, she at my sigh - ing
smil - ed, she at my sigh - ing, she at my sigh - ing
she at my sigh - ing, she at my sigh - ing
smil - - - - - - - - ed.
smil - - - - - - - - ed. But
smil - - - - - - - ed. But
she at my sigh - ing smil - - - ed.
But if you take such plea - sure, of
if you take such plea - sure, of
if you take such plea - sure, of
But if you take such plea - sure, of

hope and joy my trea - sure, by de -
hope and joy my trea - sure, by de - ceit to be -
hope and joy my trea - sure, by de - ceit to be - reave
hope and joy my trea - sure,
- ceit to be - reave me, by de - ceit to be - reave me,
- reave me, by de - ceit to be - reave me, be - reave me,
me, by de - ceit to be - reave me, to be - reave me,
by de - ceit to be - reave me,
love me and so de - ceive me. me.
love me and so de - ceive me. But me.
love me and so de - ceive me. But me.
love me and so de - ceive me. me.

No 3. WHAT CAN I DO, MY DEAREST?

cresc.
mf
-priv - ed, of those thy fair eyes, by which I still have
- - ed, of those thy fair eyes, by which I still have liv - ed, I still have liv -
-priv - ed, of those thy fair eyes, by which I still, I still have liv -
cresc.
mf
p
liv - ed? What can I do my dear - est, of
- - ed? my dear - est, of the sweet
- - ed? What can I do my dear - est, of the sweet
What can I do my dear - est, of
the sweet help de - priv - - ed? what can I do my
help de - priv - - ed? what can I do my
help, of the sweet help de - priv - - ed? what can I do my
the sweet help de - priv ed?

dear - est, of the sweet help de - priv - ed, of
dear - est, of the sweet help de - priv - ed, of
dear - est, of the sweet help de-prived, de - priv - ed, of
of the sweet help de - priv - ed, of
mf
f
those thy fair eyes, by which I still have liv - ed, I still have liv -
those thy fair eyes, by which I still have liv -
those thy fair eyes, by which I still have liv - ed, I still have liv -
those thy fair eyes, by which I still, I still have liv -
- ed, by which I still have liv - ed, I still have liv - ed?
- ed, by which I still have liv - ed?
- ed, by which I still have liv - ed?
- ed, by which I still, I still have liv - ed?

*The small notes are to be sung in the repeat.

dear sight, so full of glad -
thy dear sight, so full of
sight, so full of glad - ness, of glad -
so full of glad - ness,
ness, of glad - ness? -ness, so full of glad - ness, of
glad - ness? glad - ness, so
-ness, so full of glad - ness? -ness, so full of glad - ness, so
so full of glad - ness? so
glad - ness, so full of glad - ness.
full of glad - ness, so full of glad - ness.
full of glad - ness, so full of glad - ness.
full of glad - ness.

Nº 4. WOE AM I, MY HEART DIES.

mf
as that which on thy will — re - lies, since then I
as that which on thy will re - lies, since then I die,
as that which on thy will re - lies, since then I die, since then I —
as that which on thy will re - lies, since then I die, —
p
die, since then I die, on - ly in hope to please thee, since then I
since then I — die, on - ly in hope to please thee,
— die, since then I die, on - ly in hope to please thee, since then I
— since then I die, on - ly in hope to please thee,
die, on - ly in hope to please
since then I die, on - ly in hope, in hope to please
die, since then I die, on - ly in hope to please —
since then I die, on - ly in hope to please

thee, No grief of death though cru - - - el
thee, No grief of death though cru - - -
thee, No grief of death though cru - el
thee,
shall dis - ease me, no grief of death though cru - -
-el shall dis - ease me, no grief of death though cru -
shall dis - ease me, no grief of death though cru -
No grief of death though cru -
- - - el shall dis - ease me, yet
-el shall dis - ease me,
- - el shall dis - ease me, yet
-el shall dis - ease me, yet

shall I be tor - ment - - - ed, yet shall I
yet shall I be tor - ment - ed, tor - ment - ed,
shall I be tor - ment - ed, tor - ment - - - ed,
shall I be tor - ment - ed, yet shall I be tor-
be tor - ment - - ed, cru - el to see thee pleased
yet shall I be tor - ment - ed, tor - ment - ed,
yet shall I be tor - ment - ed, tor - ment - ed,
-ment - - ed, cru - el to
and con - tent - ed, cru - el to see thee pleased
cru - el to see thee pleased and con-
cru - el to see thee pleased and con - tent - -
see thee pleased and con - - tent -

*In this repeat the Cantus Primus and Secundus interchange parts.

Nº 5. FAREWELL, MY LOVE.

p
mf
-dained that I must leave thee, that I must
since 'tis or - dained that I must
since 'tis or-dained that I must leave thee, that I must
leave thee, since 'tis or - dained that I must
leave thee, that I must leave thee,
leave thee, must leave thee, since 'tis or -
since 'tis or-dained that I must leave thee,
leave thee, that I must leave thee, O
since 'tis or-dained that I, that I must leave thee,
-dained that I must leave thee, must leave thee, O
since 'tis or - dained that I must leave thee,

might I stay, al - though tor - ment - - - - ed, O
O might I stay, al - though tor - ment - ed,
might I stay, al - though tor - ment - - - - ed,
p
O
might I stay, al - though tor - ment - - - -
O might I stay, al - though tor - ment - - -
O might I stay, al - though tor - ment - - -
might I stay, al - though tor - ment - - -
f
- ed, the pain next death would lit - tle grieve me,
- ed, the pain next death would lit - tle grieve me,
- ed, the pain next death, the pain next death would lit - tle grieve me, the
- ed, the pain next death,

the pain would lit - tle grieve me,
the pain would lit - tle grieve me, the pain next
pain next death would lit - tle grieve me, the pain next
the pain next death would lit - tle grieve me, the pain next
the pain next death would lit - tle grieve me.
death, the pain would lit - tle grieve me.
death, the pain next death would lit - tle grieve me.
death would lit - tle grieve me.
No great - er tor - ment can be prov - ed than thus to part,
No great - er tor - ment can be prov - ed than thus to part,
No great - er tor - ment can be prov - ed than
No great - er tor - ment can be prov - ed than

than thus to part from my be-lov-
than thus to part from my be-lov-
thus to part, than thus to part from my be-lov-
thus to part,
-ed, than thus to part from my be-lov-ed.
-ed, than thus to part from my be-lov-ed.
-ed, than thus to part from my be-lov-ed.
than thus to part from my be-lov-ed.
than thus to part from my be-lov-ed.
part from my be-lov-ed.
part, than thus to part from my be-lov-ed.
my be-lov-ed.

Nº 6. SLEEP NOW, MY MUSE.

S. & B. 2376.

now, my Muse and hence - forth take thy rest, which
take thy rest, and hence-forth take thy rest, which all too
take thy rest, which all too long
now, my Muse, and hence - forth take thy rest, which
mf
all too long thy - self in vain had wast - ed,
long thy - self in vain had wast - ed, Let
thy - self in vain had wast - ed,
all too long thy - self in vain had wast - ed,
f
Let it suf - fice, let it suf -
it suf - fice, let it suf - fice,
Let it suf - fice, let it suf - fice, let
Let it suf - fice, let it suf - fice, I
p

-fice, I still must live op - pressed,
I still must live op - pressed,
it suf-fice, I still must live op - -
still must live op - pressed, and
and of my pains, and of my pains
and of my pains, and of my pains the fruit
-pressed, and of my pains
of my pains, and of my pains the
the fruit must ne'er be tast - ed, and of my pains,
must ne'er be tast - ed, and of my pains, and
the fruit must ne'er be tast - ed, and of my pains,
fruit must ne'er be tast - ed, and of my

and of my pains the fruit must ne'er be tast ed, must ne'er
of my pains the fruit must ne'er be tast-
p
the fruit must ne'er be tast - ed, the fruit must
pains the fruit must ne'er be tast -
pp
be tast - ed. Then sleep my Muse,
pp
- - ed. Then sleep my Muse,
pp
ne'er be tast - ed. Then sleep my Muse, then sleep my
pp
- - ed. Then sleep my Muse,
pp
cresc.
then sleep my Muse, Fate can - not be with -
cresc.
then sleep my Muse, Fate can - not be with -
Muse, then sleep my Muse,
cresc.
then sleep my Muse, Fate can - not be with -
cresc.

mf
-stood, it's bet - ter sleep, than wake and
-stood, it's bet - ter sleep, than
Fate can - not be with - stood, it's bet - ter sleep,
-stood, it's bet - ter sleep, than wake and do no
do no good. Then
wake and do no good. Then sleep my Muse,
than wake and do no good. Then sleep my Muse, then
good. Then
pp
sleep my Muse, then sleep my Muse, Fate can - not be with-
then sleep my Muse, Fate can - not be with-
sleep my Muse, then sleep my Muse,
sleep my Muse, then sleep my Muse, Fate can - not be with-
cresc.

Heere endeth the songs of foure parts.

Nº 7. AH, SWEET, ALAS, WHEN FIRST I SAW.

mf
Ah sweet, a - las, when first I saw those
first I saw those eyes, when first I
a - las, when first I saw
a - las, a - las, when
mf
when first I saw those eyes, those
eyes, those eyes, those eyes,
f
saw those eyes, those eyes so rich with
f
those eyes, those eyes, those
f
first I saw those eyes, those eyes, those eyes so
f
eyes, those eyes, those eyes so

f
those eyes so rich with crys - tal ma - -
crys - tal ma - jes - ty, those eyes so rich with crys - tal ma - jes -
eyes so rich with crys - tal ma - jes - ty,
rich, those eyes so rich with crys - tal
rich with crys - tal ma - jes - ty, with crys - tal ma -
p
- jes - ty, their wound - ing beau - ty
p
cresc.
- ty, their wound - ing beau - ty, their wound - ing beau -
p
cresc.
their wound - ing beau - ty, their wound - ing
p
cresc.
ma - jes - ty, their wound - ing beau - ty, their wound - ing
p
cresc.
- jes - ty, their wound - ing
p
cresc.

mf
'gan to ty - ran - nize, 'gan to
mf
- ty 'gan to ty - ran - nize, 'gan to
mf
beau - ty 'gan (then) to ty - ran - nize,
mf
beau - ty 'gan to ty -
mf
beau - ty 'gan to ty - ran - nize, 'gan to
mf
p
ty - ran - nize, And made mine eyes bleed tears
ty - ran - nize,
p
And made mine eyes bleed tears full pi -
p
- ran - nize, And made mine eyes bleed tears full
ty - ran - nize,
p

full pi - teous - ly, and made mine eyes
And made mine eyes bleed
- teous - ly, full pi - teous - ly, and made mine
pi - teous - ly,
And made mine
bleed tears full pi - teous - ly, I
tears full pi - teous - ly, I
eyes bleed tears full pi - teous - ly, I
full pi - teous - ly, full pi - teous - ly,
eyes bleed tears full pi - teous - ly,

*This note should be sung as a minim.

f
felt the wound, yet feared I not the deed, I felt the
f
felt the wound, yet feared I not the deed,
f
felt the wound, yet feared I not the deed,
f
I felt the
f
I felt the
f
wound, yet feared I not the deed,
p
yet feared I not the deed, Till
yet feared I not the deed, yet feared I not the
wound, yet feared I not the deed, yet feared I not the
wound, yet feared I not the deed, yet feared I not the deed,

p
Till ah, I found my tears did in - - ward
ah, I found my tears did in - ward bleed, my tears did in-ward
p
deed, Till ah, I found my tears did in-ward
deed,
p
Till
p
mf
bleed, did in - - ward bleed, till
bleed, my tears did in - ward bleed,
mf
bleed, till ah, I found my
p
mf
Till ah, I found my tears did in - -
mf
ah, I found my tears did in - - ward
mf

ah, I found my tears, my tears did in - - - ward
mf
till ah, I found my tears did in - - - ward
tears did in - - ward bleed, till ah, I found my
- - ward bleed,
till ah, I found my
bleed, did in - - ward bleed.
p
bleed, my tears did in - ward bleed.
p
tears, I found my tears did in - ward bleed.
p
till ah, I found my tears did in - ward bleed.
p
tears did in - - ward bleed.
p

Nº 8. MOURN NOW, MY SOUL.

f
pain, crossed are my joys, crossed are my
f
of my pain, crossed are my joys, crossed are my
f
of my pain, crossed are my joys
of my pain,
of my pain,
f
joys which hope did ev-er give, crossed are my
joys which hope did ev-er give,
which hope did ev-er give, crossed are my joys, crossed are my
f
crossed are my joys, my joys,
f
crossed are my joys,

* The G natural here and in the Altus four bars later, is evidently intended to illustrate the effect of *crossed* joy; the crossing of the parts will also be noticed as typical of the methods of the madrigalists.

* This note should be sung as a minim.

mf
dry are mine eyes, with shed-ding
mf
eyes, dry are mine eyes, with shed-ding tears
mf
with shed - ding tears in vain, dry are mine eyes, with shed-ding tears in
shed-ding tears in vain,
shed-ding tears in vain,
mf
tears in vain, with shed - ding tears in
in vain, with shed - ding tears,
vain, with shed - ding tears in vain, with
mf
with shed - ding tears in vain,
mf
with shed - ding tears in

vain, in vain, Dead is my heart, dead is my
with shed - ding tears in vain, Dead is my heart,
shed - ding tears in vain, Dead is my
with shed - ding tears in vain, Dead is my
vain, Dead is my
heart, which nev - er
which nev - er more can live, which nev - er
heart, which nev - er more can live, which nev - er
heart, which nev - er more can live, can
heart, which nev - er more

more can live, hard are my tor - ments, my tor - ments, hard are my
more can live, hard are my tor - ments, hard are my
more can live, hard are my tor - ments, hard are my
live, hard are my tor - ments, my tor - ments,
can live, hard are my tor - ments,
tor - ments, liv - ing thus in
tor - ments, hard are my tor - ments, liv - ing thus in
tor - ments, hard are my tor - ments, liv - ing thus in grief,
hard are my tor - ments, liv - ing thus in
hard are my tor - ments, liv - ing thus in

grief, Hard - er yet her heart, that yield-eth no re -
grief,
Hard - er yet her heart, that yield - - eth no re-
grief, Hard - er yet her heart, that yield - eth no re -
grief, Hard - er yet her heart, that yield-eth no re -
-lief, hard - er yet her heart, that
Hard - er yet her heart, that yield - eth
-lief, hard - er yet her heart, that yield - eth no
-lief, hard - er yet her heart, that yield - eth
-lief,

yield-eth no re-lief, hard - er yet her heart,
no re - lief, hard - er yet
re - - lief, hard - er yet her
no re - lief, hard - er yet her heart, hard - er yet
hard - er yet her heart,
that yield - eth no re - lief.
her heart, that yield-eth no re - lief.
heart, that yield - eth no re - lief.
her heart, that yield - eth no re - lief.
that yield - eth no re - lief.

No 9. SOUND OUT, MY VOICE.

(The First Part)

out my voice, with pleas-ant tunes re-cord -
with pleas-ant tunes re-cord -
out my voice, with pleas - ant tunes re - cord - -
out my voice, with pleas - ant tunes re - cord - -
out my voice, with pleas - ant tunes re-cord -
p
-ing The new de - light that love to me in-spir -
p
-ing The new de - light that love to me in - spir - -
-ing
p
-ing The new de - light that love to me in - spir - -
p
-ing The new de -
p

-eth, the new de - light that
-eth, the new de - light that love to me in - spir - eth,
p
The new de - light that love, the new de - light
-eth, the new de - light that love to
-light that love to me in spir - eth,
love to me in - spir - eth, that love to me
that love to me in - spir - eth, that love to me, to me in -
— that love to me in - spir - eth, that love to
me in - spir - eth, that love to me in -
that love to me in - spir -

*G natural may be substituted if this effect is found too harsh for modern ears.
**This note should not be sustained for more than three beats.

mf
pleased and con - tent with
mf
pleased and con - tent
that my mind de - sir - eth, my mind de - sir - eth, with
my mind de - sir - eth, my mind de - sir -
my mind de - sir eth,
that my mind de - sir - eth, my
with that my mind de - sir -
that my mind de - sir -
-eth, with that my mind
with that my mind de -

f
mind de - sir - eth. thank - ed be love, so
f
- - - eth. thank - ed be love, so
f
- eth, de - sir - eth. thank - ed be love, so
f
— de - sir - eth. thank - ed be love, so
- sir - - eth.
f
heaven - ly joys af - ford - ing, thank - ed be love, so
heaven - ly joys af - ford - ing,
heaven - ly joys af - ford - ing, thank - ed be love,
heaven - ly joys af - ford - ing, thank - ed be love, so
f
thank - ed be love, so

heaven - ly joys af - ford - ing, so heaven - ly joys af - ford - -
so heaven - ly joys af - ford - ing, so heaven - ly joys af -
so heaven - ly joys af - ford - ing, so heaven - ly
heaven - ly joys af - ford - ing, so heaven - ly joys af -
heaven - ly joys af - ford - - - ing,
- - ing, so heaven - ly
- ford - ing, so heaven - ly joys af - ford -
joys af - ford - ing, so heaven - ly joys af - ford -
- ford - ing, so heaven - ly joys af - ford -
so heaven - ly joys af - ford -

joys af - ford - - ing, so
-ing, so heaven - ly joys af - ford - -
- - - ing, so heaven - ly joys af -
-ing, so heaven - ly joys af - ford - - -
-ing, so
heaven - ly joys af - ford - - - ing.
-ing, so heaven - ly joys af - ford - - ing.
-ford - ing, so heaven - ly joys af - ford - ing.
-ing, so heaven - ly joys af - ford - ing.
heaven - ly joys af - ford - - - ing.

No. 10. SHE THAT MY PLAINTS.
(The Second Part.)

-ject - ed, she that my plaints with ri - gour
-ject - ed, she that my plaints with ri - gour long re -
-ject - ed, she that my plaints with ri - gour
-ject - ed, she that my plaints with ri - gour
she that my plaints with ri - gour long re -
long re - ject - ed,
-ject - ed, re - ject - ed, Bind -
long re - ject - ed, Bind - ing my heart,
long re - ject - ed, Bind - ing my heart,
-ject - ed, Bind - ing my heart, bind -
p

p
Bind - ing my heart, bind -
- ing my heart, bind - ing my heart, bind - ing my
bind - ing my heart,
bind - ing my heart, bind -
- ing my heart, bind - ing my
- ing my heart, with those her gold - en tress - es, with
mf
p
heart, with those her gold - en tress - es, with
bind - ing my heart, with those her gold - en tress - es, with
- ing my heart, with those her gold - en tress - es,
heart, with those her gold - en tress - es,

f
those her gold - en tress - es, with those her gold - en tress -
those her gold - en tress - es, with those her gold - en tress -
those her gold - en tress - es, with those her gold - en tress - -
with those her gold - en tress -
with those her gold - en tress - -
- es, In re - com - pense, in re - com - pense,
- es, In re - com - pense, in re - com-
- es, In re - com - pense, in
- es, In re - com - pense, in re -
- es, in re - com - pense,

in re - com - pense, in re - com - pense
-pense, in re - com - pense, in re - com-
re - com - pense, in re - com - pense, in
-com - pense, in re - com - pense, in
in re - com - pense, in re - com - pense,
p
of all my long dis-
-pense, in re - com - pense
re - com - pense of all my long dis-
re - com - pense of all my long dis-

*this note is pasted on, in the original, to correct a misprint

p
said
sigh, thy love hath me in - fect - - ed,
p
sigh, thy love hath me in - fect - - ed, said
p
sigh, thy love hath me in-fect - ed, said
p
said
p
with a sigh, thy love hath me
with a sigh, thy love hath me
with a (sweet) sigh, thy love hath me in -
with a sigh, thy love hath me in -

in - fect - - ed, thy love hath me
p
thy love hath me in -
in - fect - ed,
fect - - ed, thy love hath me in -
- fect - - ed,
f
in - fect - ed, thy love hath me in - fect -
- fect - - ed,
f
thy love hath me in - fect -
f
- fect - - ed, thy love hath me in - fect -
f
thy love hath me in - fect -
f

-ed, thy love hath me in - fect -
f
thy love hath me in -
-ed, thy love hath me in-fect -
-ed, in - fect - - ed,
-ed. thy love hath me
-ed, hath me in - fect - - - ed.
-fect - - - ed, in - fect - - ed.
- - ed, thy love hath me in-fect - ed.
thy love hath me in - fect - - ed.
in - - fect - - - ed.

Nº 11. WHAT, SHALL I PART THUS?

f
-gard - ed? from you, whom death could not dis -
-gard - ed? from you,
f
-gard - ed? from you, whom death could not dis -
f
-gard - ed? from you, whom death could not dis -
mf
f
from you, whom death could not dis -
f
-sev - er, whom death could not dis -
f
whom death could not dis - sev - er, whom
-sev - er, whom death could not dis - sev - er,
-sev - er, whom death could not dis - sev - er, whom
-sev - er, whom

p
-sev - er, whom death could not dis - sev - - er. Is
death could not dis - sev - er, dis - sev - er.
whom death could not dis - ser - - er.
death could not, whom death could not dis - sev - er.
death could not dis - sev - - - - - er.
p
faith - ful ser - vice thus cru - el - ly re - ward - - ed?
p
Is
p
Is faith - ful ser - vice thus cru - el - ly re -
p
Is faith - ful ser - vice thus cru - el - ly re - ward - ed?
p
Is faith - ful ser - vice thus cru - el -

is faith - ful ser - vice thus cru - el - ly re -
faith-ful ser-vice thus cru-el-ly re-ward - ed? re -
-ward - ed, re - ward - ed? is faith-ful ser-vice
thus cru-el - ly re-ward - ed? is faith-ful ser-vice thus cru-el -
-ly re-ward - ed?
mf
-ward - - ed? why then vain
-ward - - - ed? why then vain
thus cru - el - ly re - ward - ed? why then vain hope, a -
ly re - ward - ed? why then vain hope, a -
why then vain hope, a -

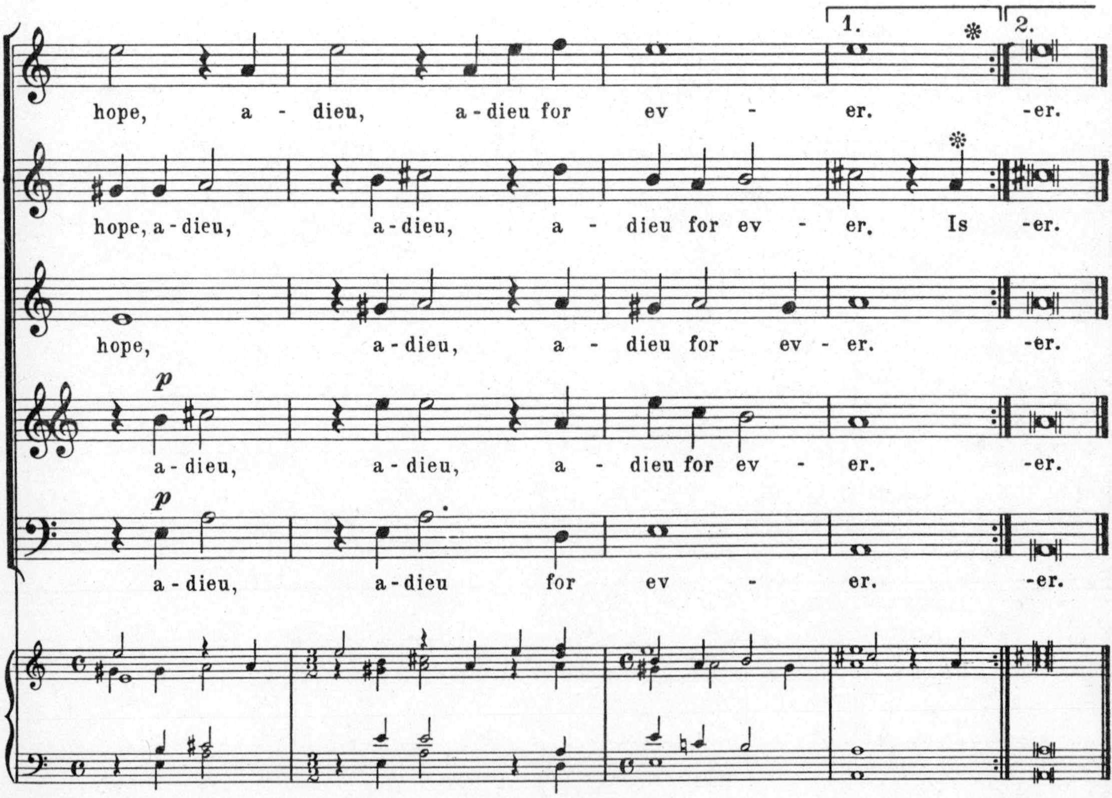

* In this repeat the Cantus Primus and Secundus interchange parts.

Nº 12. SORROW CONSUMES ME.

(The First Part.)

p
rest, and in-stead of rest, with
p
rest, and in-stead of rest, with fold-ed arms, with fold-ed
p
rest, and in-stead of rest, with fold-ed arms,
p
rest, in-stead of rest, with fold-ed arms, with
mf
p
and in-stead of rest, with fold-ed arms
p
fold-ed arms, I sad-ly sit and weep,
arms, I sad ly sit and weep,
mf
with fold-ed arms, I sad-ly sit and weep, and if I
mf
fold-ed arms, I sad-ly sit and weep, and
I sad-ly sit and weep,
mf

* *this word is printed in bracketed italics, in all parts*

see the fear-ful dreams' ef-fects,
see the fear-ful dreams' ef-fects, the
see the fear-ful dreams, the fear-ful
see the fear-ful dreams' ef-fects, the fear-ful dreams' ef-
the fear-ful dreams' ef-fects, the fear-ful
the fear-ful dreams' ef-fects, that trou-ble me.
fear-ful dreams' ef-fects, that trou-ble me.
dreams' ef-fects, the fear-ful dreams' ef-fects that trou-ble me.
-fects that trou-ble me, that trou-ble me.
dreams' ef-fects that trou-ble me, that trou-ble me.

Nº 13. O HEAVENS, WHAT SHALL I DO?

(The Second Part.)

p
cresc.
f
A - las, a - las, must I, must I my - self be
a - las, a - las, must I, must I my - self be
a - las, a - las, must I, must I my - self be
a - las, a - las, must I, must I my - self be
must I my - self be
cresc
murderer of myself? must I be murderer of my-
murderer of myself? be mur - derer of my -
murderer of my-self? must I be murderer of___ my-
murderer of my-self? must I be murderer of my-
murderer of my-self? be mur - derer of my-

-self? must I my-
-self? must I my-self be forced to ope the way? must I my-
-self? must I my-self be forced to ope the way? must I my-self
-self? must I my-self a-las be forced to ope the way? must I my-self be
-self? must I my-self a-
-self be forced to ope the way,
-self be forced to ope the way where-at my soul in wounds may
be forced to ope the way where-
forced to ope the way where-at my soul in
-las be forced to ope the way where-at my
p

p
where-at my soul in wounds may
sal - ly forth, in wounds may sal - ly forth,
-at my soul in wounds may sal - ly forth, where - at my soul in
wounds may sal - - ly forth, may sal - ly forth, where-
soul in wounds may sal - ly forth, where-at my
sal - ly forth, may sal - - ly forth?
where - at my soul in wounds may sal - ly forth?
f
wounds, where - at my soul in wounds may sal - ly forth? hard_
-at my soul, where - at my soul, may sal - ly forth? hard_
soul in wounds may sal - - - ly forth? hard_

f
hard is my hap, hard is
f
hard is my hap, hard is my
is my hap, my hap, hard is
is my hap, hard is my hap, hard
is my hap, hard is my
p
my hap, and thus in grief I die.
p
hap, and thus in grief I die.
p
my hap, and thus in grief I die.
p
is my hap, and thus in grief I die.
p
hap, and thus in grief I die.
p

Nº 14. WHY SHOULD I LOVE?

should I love since she doth prove un - grate - ful?
why should I love since she doth prove un - grate - ful?
why should I love since she doth prove un - grate - ful?
love since she doth prove un - grate - ful?
why should I love since she doth prov un - grate - ful?
since for re - ward I reap,
since for re - ward I
since for re - ward, since for
since for re - ward I reap dis - dain,
since for re -

since for re - - ward I reap nought but dis -
reap nought but dis - dain, since for re - - ward I reap dis -
re - - ward I reap nought but dis - -
since for re - ward I reap nought but dis -
- ward I reap nought but dis -
*f
-dain, I reap nought but dis - dain; love thus to
-dain, I reap nought but dis - dain;
f
-dain, I reap nought but dis - dain; love thus to
f
-dain, I reap nought but dis - dain; love thus to be re - quit -
f
-dain; love thus to be re - quit - ed,
f

* This bar is correctly transcribed from the original edition and affords a good example of the harmonic experiments of Kirbye.

be re - quit - ed, it is
it is hate - ful, it
be re-quit - ed, it is hate - ful, O
-ed, love thus to be re - quit - ed, it is
it is hate - ful,
hate - ful, and rea - son would I should not
— is hate - ful, and rea - son would I should not
it is hate - ful and rea - son would I should not
hate - ful, and rea - son would I should not
it is hate - ful, and rea - son would I should not

love in vain, I should not love in vain. yet all in
love in vain, I should not love in vain. yet
love in vain, I should not love in vain. yet all in
love in vain, not love in vain. yet all in vain,
love in vain, I should not love in vain.
vain, yet all in vain when all is out of sea - son,
all in vain, when all is out of sea - son,
vain when all is out of sea - son, for
yet all yet all in vain, in vain, for
yet all in vain when all is out of sea - son,

❋ The small notes must be sung in this repeat.

* In this repeat the Cantus Primus and Secundus interchange parts.

Nº 15. SWEET LOVE, O CEASE THY FLYING.

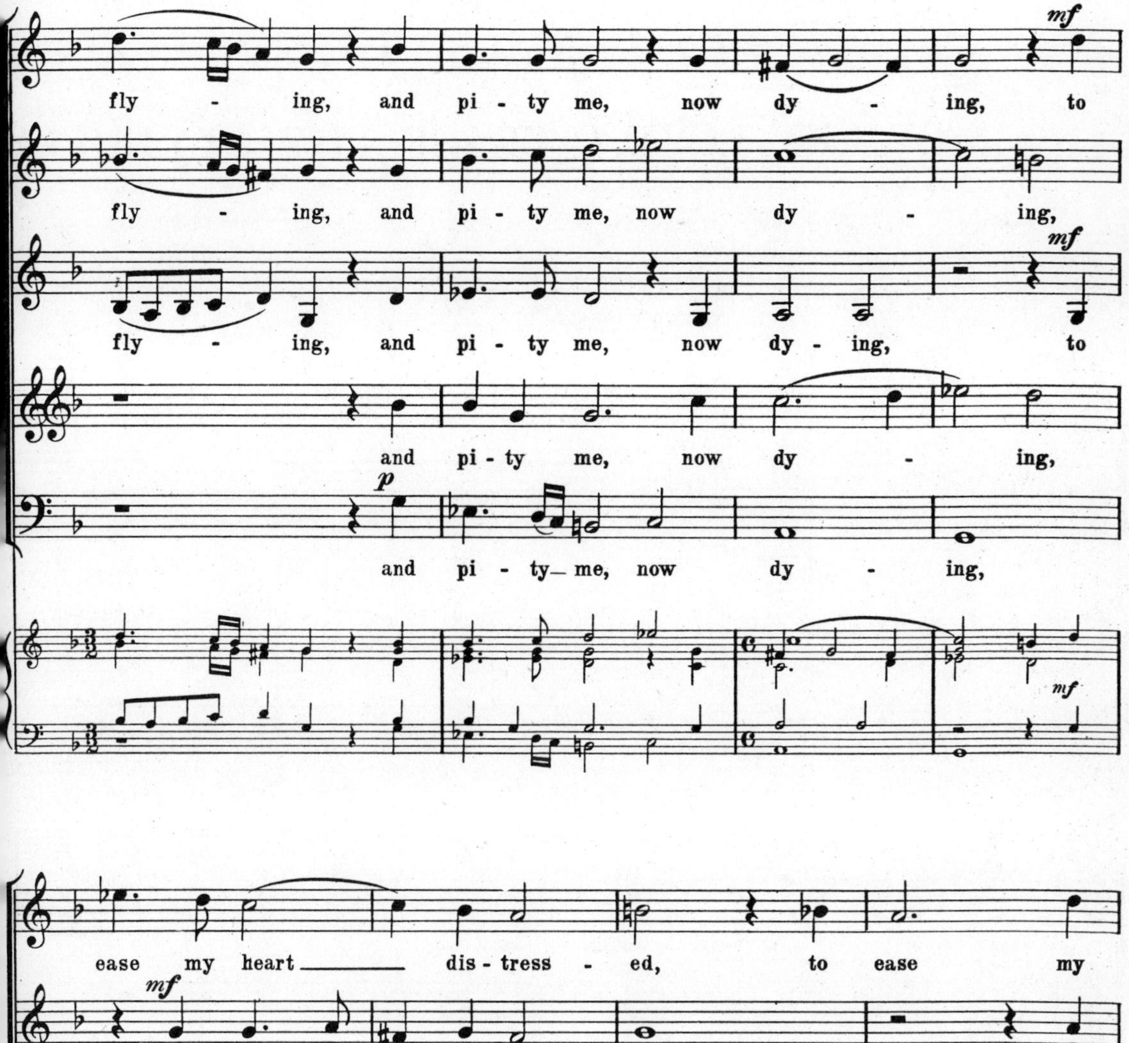
mf
fly - ing, and pi - ty me, now dy - ing, to
fly - ing, and pi - ty me, now dy - ing,
mf
fly - ing, and pi - ty me, now dy - ing, to
and pi - ty me, now dy - ing,
p
and pi - ty— me, now dy - ing,
mf
ease my heart dis - tress - ed, to ease my
mf
to ease my heart dis - tress - ed, to
ease my heart dis - tress - ed, to ease my heart, to
mf
to ease my heart dis - tress -
mf
to

* The clash of F natural against the sharp will not be found severe in the voices; the effect is repeated four bars later in the Altus & Tenor Voices.

and
and quench my rest - less burn - ing,
-turn - ing and quench my rest - less burn - ing, and quench my
-turn - ing and quench my rest - less burn - ing, and quench my
-turn - ing and quench my rest - less burn - ing, and
quench my rest - less burn - ing. That I by
and quench my rest - less burn - ing. That I by
rest - less burn - ing. That I by
rest - less burn - ing. That I by
quench my rest - less burn - ing. That I by

p
you re - dress - ed, May be re-viv-ed,
p
you re - dress - ed, May be re-viv-ed,
p cresc.
you re - dress - ed, May be re-viv - ed,
p cresc.
you re - dress - ed, May be re-viv - ed,
p cresc.
you re - dress - ed, May be re-viv-ed,
p
cresc.
cresc.
f
may be re-vived, and ho - nour you as bless - ed,
f
may be re-vived, and ho - nour you as bless - ed,
f
p
may be re-vived, and ho - nour you as bless - ed, may be re - viv - ed,
f
p
and ho - nour you as bless - ed, may be re - viv - ed,
p
may be re - vived, and
f
p

*In this repeat the Cantus Primus and Secundus interchange parts.

No. 16. THAT MUSE WHICH SUNG.

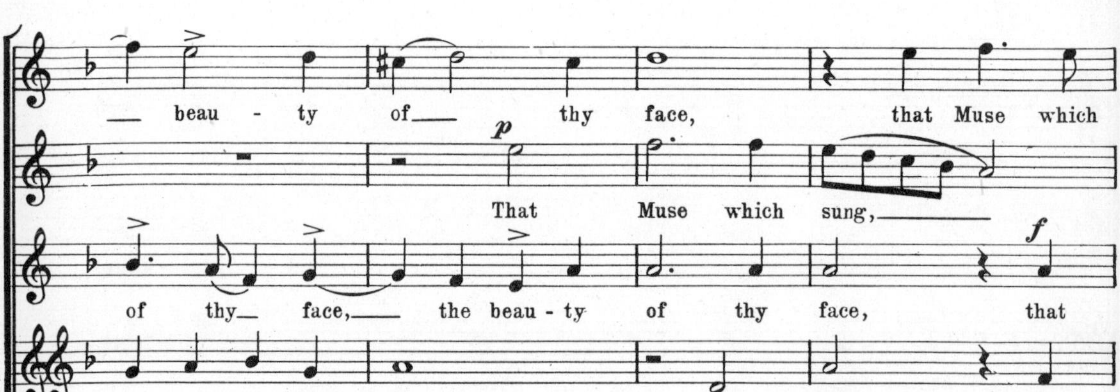

sung, that Muse which sung
that Muse which sung the beau - ty
Muse which sung the beau - ty of thy face,
sung, that Muse which sung, which sung
Muse which sung the beau - ty of thy
the beau - ty of thy face, In sweet well tun - ed songs and
of thy face,
the beau - ty of thy face, In sweet well
the beau - ty of thy face, In
face, In sweet well tun - ed

cresc.
har - mo - ny that pleas - ed, in sweet well tun - ed songs
p
cresc.
in sweet well tun - ed songs and har - mo - ny that
mf
tun - ed songs, in
cresc.
sweet well tun - ed songs and har - mo - ny that pleas - - -
cresc.
songs and har - mo - ny that pleas - - -
cresc.
mf
mf
p
and har - mo - ny that pleas - ed, if
mf
p
pleas - ed, and har - mo - ny that pleas - ed, if
sweet well tun - ed songs and har - mo - ny that pleas - ed,
mf
- ed, and har - mo - ny that pleas - ed,
p
- ed, if
p

*The bassus alone reads *those* in the original edition.

faults, that will thy worth dis - - grace.
faults, that will thy worth dis - grace.
faults, that will thy worth dis - - grace.
that will thy worth dis - grace, that will thy worth dis - grace.
faults, that will thy worth dis - - grace.
p
Yet if thou dost re - pent thee,
mf
yet
yet
yet
Yet if thou dost re - pent thee,
mf
yet

* In this repeat the Cantus Primus and Secundus interchange parts.

2.
CANTUS PRIMUS
f
-tent me, I will for-give, that mends shall well con-tent me.
CANTUS SECUNDUS.
f
-tent me, I will for-give, I will for-give that mends shall well con-tent me.
f
-tent me, I will for-give, I will for-give that mends shall well con-tent me.
f
-tent me, I will for-give that mends shall well con-tent me.
f
I will for-give, I will for-give that mends shall well con-tent me.
f

Nº 17. SEE WHAT A MAZE OF ERROR.

cresc.
-ror, and la - by-rinth of ter - ror, of ter - -
mf
-ror, and la - by-rinth of ter -
cresc.
-ror, and la - by-rinth of ter - ror, of ter - -
p cresc.
and la - by-rinth of ter-ror, and la - by-rinth of ter -
p cresc.
and la - by-rinth of ter - -
cresc.
f
-ror, my love hath trac - ed, my love hath
p
-ror, my love hath
f
p
-ror, my love hath trac - ed, my love hath
f
-ror, my love hath trac - - - ed,
f
-ror, my love hath trac - - - ed,
f
p

f
trac - - - ed, my love hath
trac - - - ed, my love hath
trac - - ed, my love hath trac - -
my love hath trac - -
my love hath trac - -
trac'd, hath trac - ed.
trac - - - ed. wretch -
p
- ed, hath trac - ed. wretch - ed I,
ed, my love hath trac - ed. wretch - ed I,
- - - - ed. wretch - ed

p
wretch - ed I, whom love
- ed I, wretch - ed I, whom love
wretch - ed I, whom
wretch - ed I, whom love pain - eth,
I, wretch - ed I, whom love
pain - eth, whom love pain - eth,
mf
pain - eth, whom love pain - eth, and true faith
mf
love pain - eth, and true faith
mf
whom love pain - eth, and true faith
pain - eth, whom love pain - eth,
mf

and true faith
on-ly gain - eth, hope ut-ter-ly dis-grac - ed, and true faith
on-ly gain-eth, hope ut-ter-ly dis-grac - - ed, and
on-ly gain - eth, hope ut-ter-ly dis-grac - ed,
and true faith
on-ly gain - eth, hope ut-ter-ly dis-grac - ed,
on-ly gain-eth, hope ut-ter-ly dis-grac - - ed,
true faith on-ly gain - eth, hope ut-ter-ly dis-grac - ed,
hope ut-ter-ly
on-ly gain - eth, hope ut-ter-ly

mf
dis - grac - ed, and by dis - dain,
hope ut - ter - ly dis - grac - ed, and by dis - dain,
hope ut - ter - ly dis - grac - ed, and by dis - dain, and by dis -
dis - grac - ed, and by dis -
dis - grac - ed, and by dis -
p
and by dis - dain de - fac - ed, and by dis - dain de - fac - -
and by dis - dain de - fac - ed, and by dis - dain de - fac - -
-dain, and by dis - dain de - fac -
-dain, and by dis - dain de - fac - ed, and by dis - dain de - fac -
-dain, and by dis - dain de - fac - -

f
-ed, and by dis - dain, and by dis-dain de - fac - ed,
f
-ed, and by dis - dain, and by dis-dain de - fac - ed,
f
-ed, and by dis - dain, and by dis - dain, and by dis-dain de - fac - ed,
f
-ed, and by dis - dain,
f
-ed, and by dis - dain,
and by dis - dain de - fac - ed.
and by dis - dain de - fac - - ed.
and by dis - dain de - fac - - ed.
and by dis - dain de - fac - - ed.
and by dis - dain de - fac - - ed.

No. 18. IF PITY REIGN WITH BEAUTY.

- sur - - ed, then may I be as - sur - ed,
be as - sur - ed, that
- ed, then may I be as - sur - ed,
then may I be as - sur - - ed, that
p
p
p
p
p
that what my harm pro - cur - ed will
what my harm pro - cur - ed, that what my harm pro - cur - ed,
that what my harm pro - cur - ed, will
what my harm pro - cur - ed, that what my harm pro - cur - ed,
mf
mf
mf

p
yield me help of du - - - ty. If pi - ty
mf
will yield me help of du - ty.
p
yield me help of du - ty. If
mf
p
will yield me help of du - ty. If
p
If
p
reign with beau - ty, if pi - ty reign with
p
If pi - ty reign with
pi - ty reign with beau - ty, if pi - ty reign with
pi - ty reign with beau - ty, if pi - ty reign with
pi - ty reign with beau - ty,

*The # to this note in the original edition was evidently intended for F in the next bar which has none.

f
-sur - ed, that
f
that what my harm pro-
f
that what my harm pro - cur - ed, that
f
- - ed, that what my harm pro-
f
-ed, that what my harm pro - cur - ed,
f
what my harm pro-cur - - ed, that what my harm pro-
-cur - ed, that what my harm pro-cur - ed,
what my harm pro - cur - ed, that what my harm pro-
-cur - ed, that what my harm pro - cur - ed,
that what my harm pro-

- cur - ed, will yield me help of du -
will yield me help of du - ty, of du -
- cur - ed, will yield me help, will yield me help of du -
will yield me help of du - ty, of du -
- cur - ed, will yield me help of du -
- ty; for wrong - ful she was nev - er, for wrong - ful she was
- ty; for wrong - ful she was nev - er, for wrong - ful she was
- ty; for wrong - ful she was nev - er, for wrong - ful she was
- ty; for wrong - ful she
- ty; for wrong - ful she was

p
nev - er. then why should I, then
p
nev - er. then why should I
p
nev - er. then why should I, then why should I, then
p
was nev - er. then why should I, then
p
nev - er. then
p
mf
why should I still in des-pair per - sev - - er? for
mf
still in des-pair per - sev - - er? for
mf
why should I still in des-pair per - sev - - er? for
mf
why should I still in des-pair per - sev - - er? for
mf
why should I, for
mf

Heere endeth the songs of five parts.

Nº 19. AH, CRUEL, HATEFUL FORTUNE.

hate - ful for - tune,
-tune, ah cru - el hate - ful for - tune, now must I
ah cru - el hate - ful for - tune, now
for - tune, now must I death
ah cru - el hate - ful for - tune, now must I
now must I death im - por -
now must I death im - por - - -
death im - por - tune, now must I death im - por -
must, now must I death im - por -
- im - por - tune, now must I death im - por -
death im - por - tune, now must I death im - por -
-tune, now must I death im - por -

-tune, since that I am of all my hope de - priv -
-tune, since that I am of all my hope de-priv - -
-tune, since that I am of all my hope de - priv -
-tune, since that I am of all my hope de - priv -
-tune,
-tune,
- - ed, nor but for
- - ed, nor but for
- - ed, nor but for sor - row, nor but for
- ed, nor but for sor - row,
nor but for sor - row,
nor but for sor - row,

* This note should be sung as a crotchet.

rest for my con - tent - ment,
on - ly this hope doth rest for my con -
rest for my con - tent - ment, on - ly this hope doth rest for my con -
rest for my con - tent - ment, on - ly this hope doth rest for
rest for my con - tent - ment,
on - ly this hope doth rest for my con -
mf
that for - tune tired will yield me some a - mend - ment,
- tent - ment, that for - tune tired will
- tent - ment, that for - tune tired will
my con - tent - ment, that for - tune tired,
that for - tune tired will yield me some a - mend -
- tent - ment, that for - tune

that for - tune tired will yield me some a - mend -
yield me some a - mend - ment, that for - tune tired will
yield me some a - mend - ment, that for - tune tired will
that for - tune tired will yield me some a - mend-ment some
-ment, that for - tune tired,
tired, that for - tune tired will yield me some a - mend
-ment, that for - tune tired will yield me some a - mend - ment,
yield me some a - mend - ment, some a - mend - - ment, on -
yield me some a - mend - ment, on -
a-mend - ment, that for - tune tired will yield me some a-mend - ment,
that for - tune tired will yield me some a - mend - ment, on -
-ment, on -
p
p
p
p
p

p
on - ly this hope doth rest for my con -
-ly this hope doth rest for my con - tent - ment on - ly this hope doth rest for my con -
-ly this hope doth rest for my con - tent - ment on - ly this hope doth rest for my con -
p
on - ly this hope doth rest for my con -
-ly this hope doth rest for my con - tent - ment
-ly this hope doth rest for my con - tent - ment
mf
-tent - ment, that for - tune tired will
-tent - ment, that for - tune tired will yield me some a - mend -
-tent - ment, that for - tune tired will
-tent - ment, that for - tune tired will yield me some a - mend - ment, some
that for - tune tired,
that for - tune tired will yield me some a - mend -

yield me some a - mend - ment, that
-ment, that for - tune tired will yield me some a - mend -
yield me some a - mend - ment, that
a - mend - ment, that for - tune tired will yield me some a - mend -
that for - tune tired will yield me some a - mend -
-ment, will
for - tune tired will yield me some a - mend - ment.
-ment, will yield me some a - mend - ment.
for - tune tired will yield me some a - mend - ment.
ment, that for - tune tired will yield me some a - mend - ment.
ment, will yield me some a - mend - ment.
yield me some a - mend - ment.

Nº 20. I LOVE, ALAS, YET AM I NOT BELOVED.

-ed, I love, a - las, yet am I not be -
-ed, I love, a - las, yet am I not be -
-ed, I love, a - las, I love, a - las,
I love, a - las, I love, a - las,
-ed, I love, a - las, yet
-ed, I love, a - las,
-lov - ed, yet am I not be - lov - ed, my
-lov - ed, yet am I not be lov - ed,
yet am I not be - lov - ed, my
yet am I not be - lov - ed,
am I not be - lov - ed, my suits are all re -
yet am I not be - lov - ed, my suits are all re -

suits are all re - ject - ed, my suits are all re -
mf
my suits are all re - ject - ed,
suits are all re - ject - ed, my suits are all re -
mf
my suits are all re - ject - ed,
-ject - ed, re - ject - ed, re - ject - ed,
-ject - ed, my suits are all re - ject - ed,
-ject - ed, and all my looks sus - pect - - ed.
and all my looks sus - pect - ed.
-ject - ed, and all my looks sus - pect - - ed.
and all my looks sus - pect - ed, sus - pect - ed.
and all my looks sus - pect - - - ed.
and all my looks sus - pect - - - ed.

f
Ex - pe - ri - ence now too late hath
Ex - pe - ri - ence now too late hath
Ex - pe - ri - ence
Ex - pe - ri - ence now too late hath
Ex - pe - ri - ence now too late hath
Ex - pe - ri - ence now too late hath
prov - ed, now too late hath prov - ed
prov - ed
now too late hath prov - ed
— prov - ed, now too late hath prov - ed that 'twas in
prov - ed that 'twas in vain that
prov - ed that 'twas in vain that erst I
p

p
that 'twas in vain that erst I
that 'twas in vain that erst I lov - ed,
that 'twas in vain that
vain that erst I lov - ed,
erst I lov - ed, that 'twas in
lov - ed,
lov - ed, that 'twas in vain that
that 'twas in vain that erst I
erst I lov - ed, that 'twas in vain,
that 'twas in vain, that 'twas in
vain that erst I lov - ed,
that 'twas in vain that erst I lov - ed,

n this repeat the Cantus Primus and Secundus interchange parts.

Nº 21. MUST I PART, O MY JEWEL?

must I part, O my Jew -
hap - less, must I
hap - less, must I part, O my
- less, must
must I part, O my Jew - el, hap -
must I part, O my Jew - el,
-el, hap - less,
part, O my Jew - el,
Jew - el, hap - less,
I part, O my Jew - el, hap -
- less, must I part, O my Jew -
hap - less, must I part, O my

cresc.
hap - less, from my fair sun, whose beams me
hap - - less, from my fair sun, whose beams me
hap - less, from my fair sun, whose beams me
-less, hap - less, from my fair sun, whose beams me
-el, hap - less, from my fair sun, whose beams me
Jew - el, hap - less,
f
p
nou - rish, whose beams me nou - - rish? A - -
nou - rish, whose beams me nou - rish? A -
nou - rish, me nou - - rish? A - -
nou - rish, whose beams me nou - - rish? A - -
nou - rish, whose beams me nou - rish? A - las,
whose beams me nou - - rish? A - -

mf
-las, who now com - fort - eth? A -
-las, A - - las,
-las, who now com - fort - eth? A - -
-las, who now com - fort - eth? A - -
who now com - fort -
-las, who now com - fort - eth?
- - las, or doth me che - rish?
who now com - fort - eth? or doth me che - rish?
-las, who now com-fort - eth? or doth me che - rish?
-las, who now com - fort - eth? or doth me che - rish?
-eth? who now com - fort - eth? or doth me che - rish?
or doth me che - rish?

p
pain - ed with grief so cru -
p
pain - ed with grief so
p
pain - ed with grief so
p
pain - ed with grief so cru - - el,
p
pain - ed with grief so cru -
p
cresc.
- el, O if it
cru - el, O if it
cru - el, O if it
O if it
- - el, O
O
cresc.

*This note is misprinted B in the original edition *in the cantus secundus part only.*

*In this repeat the Cantus Primus and Secundus interchange parts.

Nº 22. UP THEN, MELPOMENE.

(The First Part.)

Words by Sir Philip Sidney. (1554–1586)

mf
f
-ing, of mourn-ing, such cause of mourn-ing
mourn-ing, such cause of mourn-ing nev-er hadst
cause of mourn-ing, such cause of mourn-ing
-ing, such cause of mourn-ing, such cause of mourn-ing nev-
cause of mourn-ing, such cause of mourn-ing nev-
such cause of mourn-ing nev-er
nev-er hadst a-fore. Up, gris-ly
a-fore. Up, gris-ly
nev-er hadst a-fore. Up, gris-ly
-er hadst a-fore. Up gris-ly ghosts,
-er hadst a-fore. Up,
hadst a-fore. Up, gris-ly

ghosts, and up, my rue - ful
ghosts, and up, my rue - ful
ghosts, and up, my rue - ful
up, gris - ly ghosts, and up, my rue - ful
gris - ly ghosts, and up, my rue - ful rhyme,
ghosts, and up my rue - ful
p
rhyme, Mat - ter of mirth now shalt thou have no
rhyme, Mat - ter of mirth now shalt thou have no
rhyme, Mat - ter of mirth now shalt thou have no
rhyme, Mat - ter of mirth now shalt thou have no
rhyme.

*This note should be sung as a dotted minim.

❊ This note is misprinted A in the original edition.

- do my dear a - las is dead, Di - do my dear a -
mf
Di - do my dear a - las is dead,
mf
dead, Di - do my dear a - las is
mf
Di - do my dear a - las is
dear a - las is dead,
-las is dead,
mf

dim.
-las, a - las is dead, Di - do my
dim.
Di - do my dear a -
dead, Di - do my
dim.
dead, Di - do my dear a - las is dead, a -
mf
dim.
Di - do my dear a - las is dead, a -
mf
dim.
Di - do my dear a - las is
dim.

dear a - las is dead, dead
-las is dead, dead and li - eth
dear a - las is dead,
-las is dead, dead and li - eth wrapped in
- las is dead,
dead, dead and li - eth
and li - eth wrapped in lead, dead and li - eth
wrapped in lead, dead and li - eth wrapped in lead, and
dead and li - eth wrapped in lead, dead and
lead, dead and li - eth wrapped in lead,
dead and li - eth wrapped in lead, and li - eth
wrapped in lead, dead and li - eth
cresc.

— wrapped in lead.
li - eth wrapped in lead.
O hea - vy hearse!
dim.
li - eth wrapped in lead.
O hea - vy
molto dim.
O hea - vy hearse! O hea - vy
molto dim.
wrapped in lead. O hea - vy hearse!
dim.
wrapp - ed in lead. O
O hea - vy hearse! Let stream - ing tears be
O hea - vy hearse! Let stream - ing tears be
hearse! O hea - vy hearse! Let stream - ing
hearse! O hea - vy hearse!
O hea - vy hearse! Let stream - ing tears be
hea - vy hearse!

pour - ed out in store,
pour - ed out in store,
cresc.
tears be pour - ed out in store, let stream - ing tears be pour - ed out in
cresc.
Let stream - ing tears be pour - ed out in
cresc.
pour - ed out in store, let stream - ing tears be pour
cresc.
Let stream - ing tears be pour - ed out in
cresc.
mf
let stream - ing tears be pour - ed out in
mf
let stream - ing tears be pour - ed out in
mf
store, let stream - ing tears be pour - ed
mf
store, let stream - ing tears be pour - ed out in
ed out in store,
store,
mf

store,
store,
out in store, be pour - ed out in store. O
store let stream - ing tears be pour - ed out in store. O
let stream - ing tears be pour - ed out in store. O
let stream - ing tears be pour - ed out in store. O
care - ful verse! O care - ful verse!
care - ful verse! O care - ful verse!
care - ful verse! O care - - ful verse!
care - ful verse! O care - ful verse!
care - ful verse! O care - - ful verse!
care - ful verse! O care - ful verse!

Nº 23. WHY WAIL WE THUS?

(The Second Part.)

Words by Sir Philip Sidney (1554-1586)

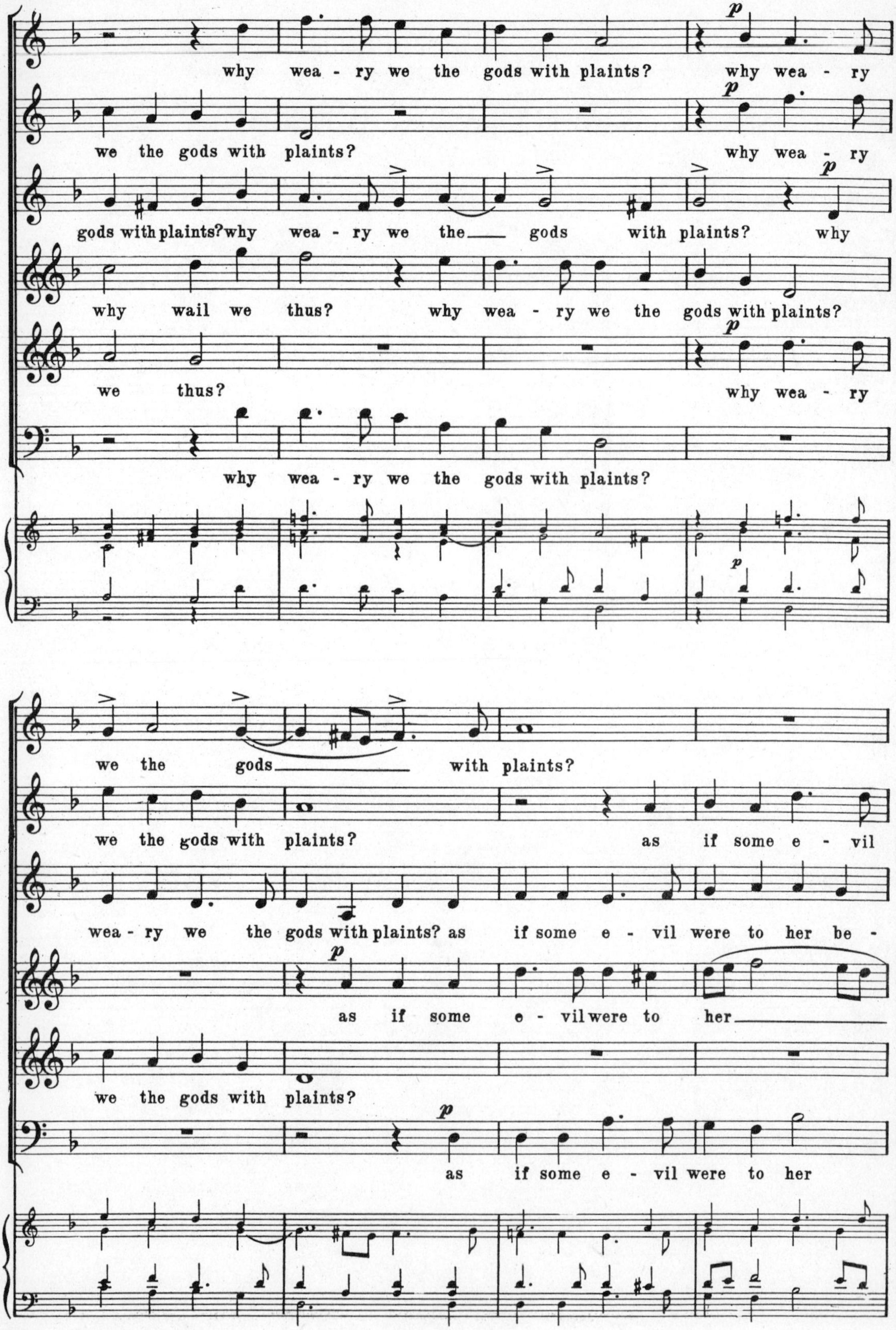
why wea - ry we the gods with plaints? why wea - ry
we the gods with plaints? why wea - ry
gods with plaints? why wea - ry we the gods with plaints? why
why wail we thus? why wea - ry we the gods with plaints?
we thus? why wea - ry
why wea - ry we the gods with plaints?
we the gods with plaints?
we the gods with plaints? as if some e - vil
wea - ry we the gods with plaints? as if some e - vil were to her be -
as if some e - vil were to her
we the gods with plaints?
as if some e - vil were to her

as if some e - vil were to her be -
were to her be - tight,
- tight, as if some e - vil were to her be -
be - tight, as if some e - vil were to her be -
as if some e - vil were to her be -
be - tight,
ff
- tight, She reigns a god - dess now a - mong the
She reigns a god - dess now a - mong the
- tight, She reigns a god - dess now a - mong the
- tight, She reigns a god - dess now a - mong the
- tight, She reigns a god - dess now a - mong the
She reigns a god - dess now a - mong the

the notes and words between the signs are pasted on, in the original, to conceal a misprint

saint of shep - herds' light, of shep - herds'
that whil-om was the saint of shep-herds' light, of shep - herds'
light, that whil-om was the saint of shep - herds'
light, that whil-om was the saint of shep - herds' light,
that whil-om was the saint of shepherds'
whil-om was the saint of shep-herds' light,
f
light, and is in-stall - ed now in hea-ven's height,
light, and is in-stall - ed now in hea-ven's height,
light, and is in-stall - ed now in heaven's height, and
and is in-stall - ed now in heaven's height,
light, and is in -

and is in - stall - ed now in hea - ven's height.
and is in - stall - ed now in hea - ven's height.
is in - stall - ed now in hea - ven's height.
and is in - stall - ed now in — heaven's height.
- stall - ed now in hea - ven's height.
and is in - stall - ed now in hea - ven's height.
p
I see thee, bless - ed soul, I see
I see thee, bless - ed soul, I see
I see thee, bless - ed soul, I see, I see thee, bless - ed
I see thee, bless - ed soul, I see, I see thee, bless - ed
I see thee, bless - ed soul, I see, I see thee, bless - ed
I see thee, bless - ed

*time signature ... etc.

walk in E - ly - si - an fields, E -
walk in E - ly - si - an fields so free, E -
soul, I see walk in E - ly - si - an fields so free, E -
soul, I see walk in E - ly - si - an, walk in E -
soul, I see walk in E - ly - si - an
soul, I see walk in E - ly - si - an fields so free, E -
(♩ = ♩)
f
-ly - si - an fields so free. O hap - py hearse!
-ly - si - an fields so free. O hap - py hearse! O hap - py
-ly - si - an fields so free. O hap - py hearse!
-ly - si - an fields so — free. O hap - py
fields so free, so free. O hap - py hearse! O
-ly - si - an fields so free. O

p
O hap - py hearse! might I once come to thee, O that I
hearse! O hap - py hearse! might I
O hap - py hearse! might I once come to thee O that I
hearse! O hap - py hearse! O that I might come to thee,
hap - py hearse! might I once come to thee, O that I might, O
hap - py hearse! might I once come to
might, O that I might O
once come to thee O that I might, O joy -
might, might I once come to thee, O that I
might I once come to thee, O that I might,
that I might, O joy -
thee, O that I might, O that I might,
f

joy - ful verse! O joy - ful
- - - ful verse! O joy-ful verse!
might, O joy - - ful verse! O joy - - - ful
O joy - - ful verse! O
- - ful verse! O
O joy - - - ful
verse! O joy - - - - ful verse!
O joy - - ful verse! O joy - ful verse!
verse! O joy - - ful verse! O joy - ful verse!
joy - - ful verse! O joy - ful verse!
joy - ful verse! O joy - - - ful verse!
verse! O joy - - ful verse!

Nº 24. SLEEP NOW, MY MUSE.

and hence - forth take thy rest, sleep now, my
and hence - forth take thy rest,
hence - forth take thy rest, sleep
rest, and hence - forth
rest, and hence - forth take thy
Sleep now, my Muse,
Muse, and hence - forth take thy
and hence - forth take thy rest,
now, my Muse, and hence - forth take thy
take thy rest, hence - forth take thy
rest, and hence-forth take thy rest,
and hence - forth take thy

mf
rest, which all too long,
mf
— which all too long, which all too long
mf
rest, which all too long, which all too
mf
rest, which all too long, thy-self in vain had wast -
mf
— which all too long, thy - self in
mf
rest, which all too long,
mf
which all too long thy - self in vain had wast - ed, had
— thy - self in vain had wast - ed, had wast -
long thy - self in vain had wast -
- - ed, thy - self in vain had wast -
vain had wast - ed, thy - self in vain had
— thy - self in vain had wast - - -

p
wast - ed: Let it suf - fice, let it suf -
p
- ed: Let it suf - fice, let it suf - fice,
p
- ed: Let it suf - fice, let it suf - fice,
p
- ed: Let it suf - fice, I still must live op -
p
wast - ed: Let it suf - fice, I still must live op -
- ed:
- fice, let it suf - fice, I
I still must live op - pressed, I
I still must live op - pressed, I still must live
- pressed, let it suf - fice, I still must live
- pressed, let it suf - fice,
p
Let it suf - fice, I still must

cresc.
still must live op - pressed, and
still must live op - - pressed,
op - - pressed, op - pressed,
cresc.
I still must live op - pressed, and of my
I still must live op - pressed,
live op - - pressed,
cresc.
of my pains, the fruit must ne'er be
cresc.
and of my pains, the fruit must
cresc.
and of my pains, the fruit must ne'er be tast - ed, be
pains, the fruit must ne'er be

cresc.
tast - ed, and of my pains,
ne'er be tast - ed, and of my pains,
tast - - ed, and of
tast - - ed, and of my pains, and
and of my pains, and
and of my pains, and of my
and of my pains, the fruit must ne'er be
and of my pains,
my pains, the fruit must ne'er be tast - ed,
of my pains, the fruit must ne'er be tast - ed, be
of my pains, the fruit must ne'er be
pains, the fruit must

tast - - ed, the fruit must ne'er be tast - ed.
the fruit must ne'er be tast - - ed.
the fruit must ne'er be tast - ed.
tast - ed, must ne'er be tast - ed.
tast - ed, must ne'er be tast - ed.
ne'er be tast - - - ed.
p
Then sleep, my Muse,
mf
Fate can - not be with-
Then sleep, my Muse, then sleep, my Muse,
Then sleep, my Muse,
Then sleep, my Muse, then sleep, my Muse,
Then sleep, my Muse,

-stood, It's bet - ter sleep,
-stood, Fate can - not be with - stood, It's bet - ter sleep,
-stood, Fate can - not be with - stood, It's bet - ter sleep, it's bet - ter
mf
Fate can - not be with - stood, It's bet - ter
-stood, It's bet - ter
mf
Fate can - not be with - stood, It's bet - ter
than wake and do no good.
it's bet - ter sleep,
pp
Then sleep, my
sleep, than wake and do no good. Then sleep, my
sleep, it's bet - ter sleep, than wake and do no good. Then sleep, my
sleep, than wake and do no good.
sleep, Then sleep, my

pp
Then sleep, my Muse, Fate can-not be with-stood, Fate
Muse,
Fate can-not be with-stood,
Muse, then sleep, my Muse, Fate can-not be with-stood, Fate
Muse, then sleep, my Muse, Fate
Then sleep, my Muse, Fate can-not be with-stood,
Muse, Fate
can-not be with-stood, It's bet-ter sleep,
It's bet-ter sleep,
can-not be with-stood, It's bet-ter sleep, it's bet-ter
can-not be with-stood, It's bet-ter
It's bet-ter
can-not be with-stood, It's bet-ter

it's bet - ter sleep, than wake and
than wake and do no good, do no
sleep, than wake and do no good, than wake and
sleep, it's bet - ter sleep, than wake and do no good, and do no good,
sleep, than wake and do no good,
sleep, than wake and
pp
do no good, and do no good.
pp
good, than wake and do no good.
pp
do no good, and do no good.
pp
than wake and do no good.
pp
than wake and do no good.
pp
do no good.
pp

A Madrigal by George Kirbye.

included by Thomas Morley as No. 20 in
"THE TRIUMPHS OF ORIANA"
(1601)

Edited by EDMUND H. FELLOWES.
Revised by Thurston Dart.

WITH ANGEL'S FACE AND BRIGHTNESS.
(BRIGHT PHOEBUS GREETS.)

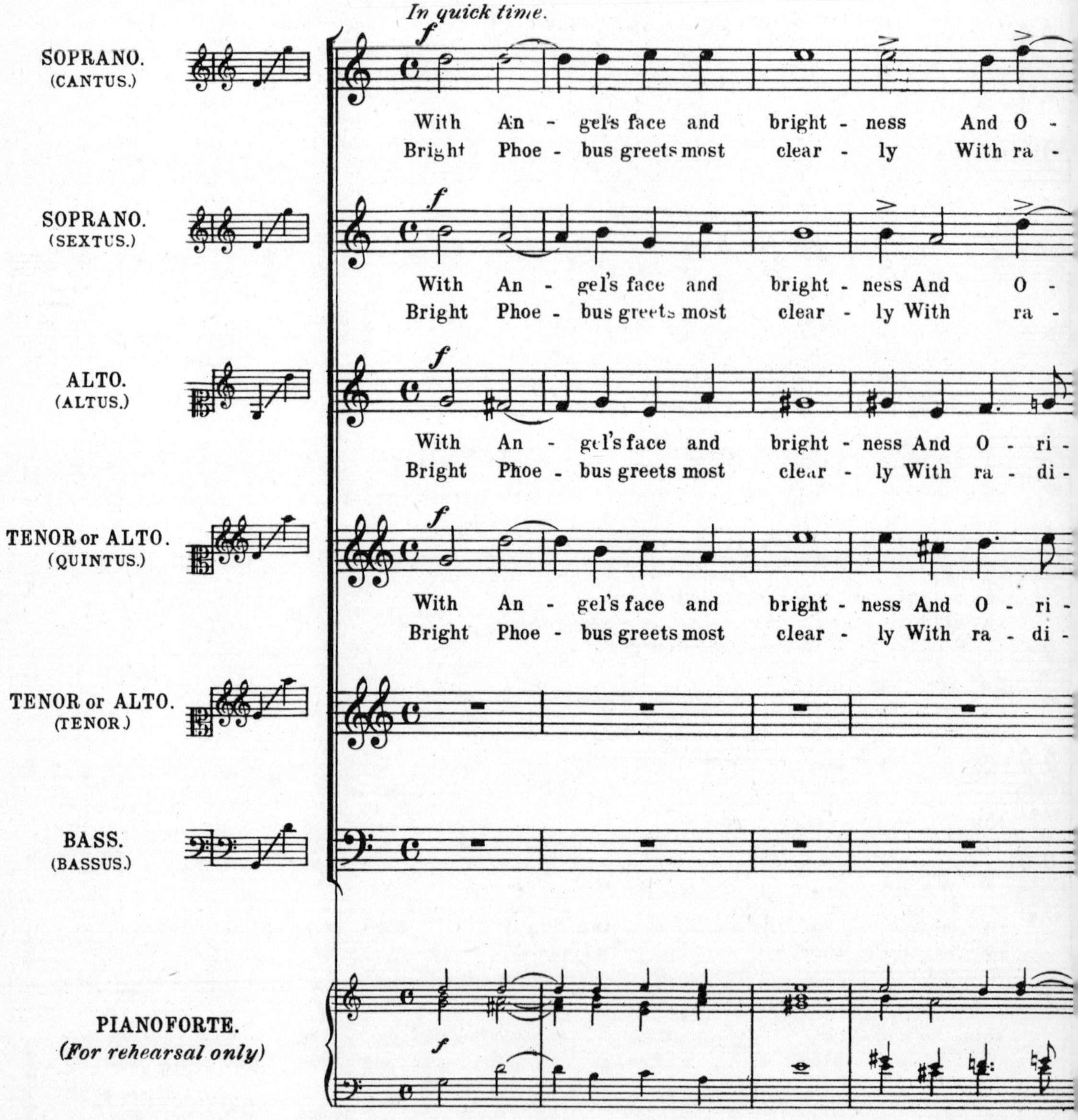

Note. The two alternative versions of the words, each dating from 1601, are printed here with the music.

-ri-ent hue, fair O-ri-a-na, fair O-ri-a-na, fair O-ri-a-na
-di-ant beams fair O-ri-a-na, fair O-ri-a-na, fair O-ri-a-na
-ri-ent hue, fair O-ri-a-na, fair O-ri-a-na, fair O-ri-
-di-ant beams fair O-ri-a-na, fair O-ri-a-na, fair O-ri-
-ent hue, fair O-ri-a-na, fair O - ri - a-na, fair O-ri-
-ant beams fair O-ri-a-na, fair O - ri - a-na, fair O-ri-
-ent hue, fair O-ri-a-na, fair O-ri-a-na, fair O-ri-a-na
-ant beams fair O-ri-a-na, fair O-ri-a-na, fair O-ri-a-na
Fair O-ri-a-na, fair O-ri-a-na, fair O-ri-
Fair O-ri-a-na, fair O-ri-a-na, fair O-ri-
Fair O-ri-a-na
Fair O-ri-a-na
shin - ing, With nim-ble foot she tripped, with nim-ble foot she
sit - ting, Her ap-ple Ve-nus yields, her ap-ple Ve-nus
-a-na shin - ing, With nim-ble foot she tripped o'er hills and mount-ains,
-a-na sit - ting. Her ap-ple Ve-nus yields as best be-fit-ting,
-a-na shin-ing, o'er
-a-na sit-ting. as
shin - ing, With nim-ble foot she trip-ped o'er
sit - ting. Her ap-ple Ve-nus yield-eth as
-a-na shin - ing, With nim-ble foot she trip - ped o'er hills and mount -
-a-na sit - ting, Her ap-ple Ve-nus yield - eth as best be-fit -
shin - ing, With nim-ble foot she trip-ped,
sit - ting, Her ap-ple Ve-nus yield-eth,
p

*This note should be sung as a crotchet.

fount - ains, Di - a - na's fount - - - ains.
trea - sures, rich Plu - to leaves his trea - sures,
-a - na's fount - ains, Di - a - na's fount - - ains.
leaves his trea - sures, leaves his trea - - sures,
- na's fount - ains, Di - a - na's fount - ains.
his trea - sures, leaves his trea - - - sures,
-a - na's fount - ains, Di - a - na's fount - - - ains.
leaves his trea - sures, leaves his trea - - - sures,
fount - ains, Di - a - na's fount - - - ains.
trea - sures, leaves his trea - - sures,
-a - na's fount - ains, Di - a - na's fount - - - ains.
leaves his trea - sures, leaves his trea - - sures,
p
This is that maid - en Queen of the fai - ry land
And Pros - er - pine glad runs in her best ar - ray,
p
This is that maid - en Queen of the fai - ry land
And Pros - er - pine glad runs in her best ar - ray,
p
This is that maid - en Queen of the fai - ry land
And Pros - er - pine glad runs in her best ar - ray,
p
With Nymphs
p
With Nymphs
p

p
With scep - tre in her hand, with scep - tre
Nymphs deck her crown with bay, Nymphs deck her
With scep - tre in her hand, with
Nymphs deck her crown with bay, Nymphs
With scep - tre in her hand, with scep - tre in her
Nymphs deck her crown with bay, Nymphs deck her crown with
With scep - tre in her hand, with scep - tre
Nymphs deck her crown with bay, Nymphs deck her
scep - tre in her hand, with scep - tre in
deck her crown with bay, Nymphs deck her crown
scep - tre in her hand, with scep - tre
deck her crown with bay, Nymphs deck her
in her hand.
crown with bay.
scep - tre in her hand.
deck her crown with bay.
hand. The Fauns and Sa - tyrs danc - ing,
bay. Her feet are li - ons kiss - ing,
in her hand. The Fauns and Sa - tyrs danc - ing
crown with bay. Her feet are li - ons kiss - ing:
her hand. The Fauns and Sa - tyrs danc - ing,
with bay. Her feet are li - ons kiss - ing,
in her hand. The Fauns and Sa - tyrs danc - ing
crown with bay. Her feet are li - ons kiss - ing:
f

The Fauns and Sa - tyrs danc - ing did show their nim - ble
Her feet are li - ons kiss - ing: No joy can there be
the Fauns and Sa - tyrs danc - ing
her feet are li - ons kiss - ing:
did show their nim - ble
No joy can there be
light - ness, did show their nim - ble light - ness:
miss - ing, no joy can there be miss - ing.
did show their nim - ble light - ness:
No joy can there be miss - ing.
light - ness:
miss - ing.
Fair
Now

p
and brought their
and swells with
Na - is and the Nymphs did leave their bow - ers.
Thet - is leaves the mer - maids' tunes ad - mir - ed.
Na - is and the Nymphs did leave their bow - ers, and brought their
Thet - is leaves the mer - maids' tunes ad - mir - ed, and swells with
bas - kets full of herbs and flow - ers.
pride to see this Queen de - sir - ed.
f
Then sang the

shep - herds and Nymphs of Di - a - na, Nymphs of Di -
shep - herds and Nymphs of Di - a - na, Nymphs of Di -
shep - herds and Nymphs of Di - a - na, Nymphs of Di -
shep - herds and Nymphs of Di - a - na, and Nymphs of Di -
shep - herds and Nymphs of Di - a - na, Nymphs of Di -
shep - herds and Nymphs of Di - a - na, Nymphs of Di -
- a - na, Long live fair O - ri - a - na,
- a - na, Long live fair O - ri -
- a - na, Long live fair
- a - na, Long live fair O - ri - a - na, fair O - ri -
- a - na, Long live fair O - ri - a - na,
- a - na, Long live fair O - ri - a - na,

long live fair O - ri - a - na, long
- a - na, long live fair O - ri - a -
O - ri - a - - na, fair O - ri - a - na,
- a - na, long live fair O - ri - a - na,
long live fair O - ri - a - na, fair
long live fair O - ri - a - na, long live fair
live fair O - ri - a - na, long live fair O - ri -
- na, long live fair O - ri - a - na, long
long live fair O - ri - a - na, long
fair O - ri - a - na, long live fair
O - ri - a - na, long live fair O - ri - a - na,
O - ri - a - na, long live fair O - ri - a - na,

Lowe and Brydone (Printers) Limited, London

INDEX

THE ENGLISH MADRIGALISTS

Edited by

EDMUND H. FELLOWES

Revised by Thurston Dart

25

FRANCIS PILKINGTON

First Set of

MADRIGALS AND PASTORALS

of 3, 4, and 5 Parts

(1613)

STAINER & BELL, LTD.,
29 NEWMAN STREET, LONDON, W.1

MADE IN GREAT BRITAIN

REVISER'S NOTE

The text has been checked and corrected from the British Museum copy of, the original edition. I am grateful to Mr Gerald Hendrie for his help with this revision.

THURSTON DART

PREFACE TO VOLUME XXV.

IT has not been thought necessary to reprint in each volume of this Series the full explanation of the methods adopted by the Editor, especially as the Preface to Volume I. is published separately, and can be obtained separately by those who have not a copy of that volume. It is very important, however, to emphasize that a thorough grasp of the principles which are explained in detail in that treatise is absolutely indispensable for a clear understanding and practical use of this Edition, and particular attention is directed to the paragraph on Rhythm and Barring.

The musical illustrations there employed are drawn exclusively from the works of Thomas Morley, but the principles which they illustrate apply to the whole of this Series.

The following points are fully dealt with under separate headings :—

1. Clefs.
2. Words.
3. Expression.
4. Rhythm and Barring.
5. Repeat Marks.
6. Time-signatures.
7. Key-signatures.
8. Accidentals.
9. Pianoforte Score.

Though I have used every endeavour to reproduce an accurate version of the original text throughout this Series, I am aware that in a work of this magnitude it is almost inevitable that some misprints should escape detection in reading the proofs. I shall be glad to have any such misprints brought to my notice, so that they may be corrected in future editions. I shall also welcome any information as to the authorship of any of the lyrics not hitherto identified.

Francis Pilkington may have owed something to the influence of Thomas Bateson, since both held official positions—one as Precentor and the other as Organist of Chester Cathedral.

The connexion of Francis with the Lancashire family of Pilkington cannot be traced, although it seems probable that he must have belonged to it. His father was at one time in the service of the Stanleys. Francis was ordained by the Bishop of Chester in 1614 and became a Minor Canon of the Cathedral a few years after Bateson had gone to Dublin as Organist of Christ Church Cathedral. He became Precentor of Chester Cathedral in 1623 and at the same time was the incumbent of Holy Trinity Church in Chester. His first set of madrigals was dated September 25th, 1612, and was published in 1613, he being resident in "my mansion in the monastery of Chester" at that time, although it was quite a year before his ordination. Possibly he held the position of lay clerk, for he had made his mark as a musician some years earlier, his book of lute-songs having appeared as early as 1605. He was a notable Lutenist.

The date of Pilkington's birth remains unknown; it may approximately be conjectured as being between 1560 and 1565. He took the Mus.Bac. degree at Oxford in 1595, having at that time studied music for sixteen years. He died in 1638.

EDMUND H. FELLOWES.

THE CLOISTERS,
WINDSOR CASTLE,
July 30th, 1920.

LYRICS

Set by Francis Pilkington

In his First Set of Madrigals and Pastorals

1613

I.

See where my love a-maying goes, with sweet Dame Flora sporting,
She most alone with nightingales in woods' delights consorting.
Turn again, my dearest, the pleasant'st air's in meadows,
Else by the rivers let us breathe, and kiss amongst the willows.

II.

I follow, lo, the footing
Still of my lovely cruel,
Proud of herself that she is beauty's jewel;
And fast away she flieth,
Love's sweet delight deriding,
In woods and groves sweet Nature's treasure hiding.
Yet cease I not pursuing,
But since I thus have sought her,
Will run me out of breath till I have caught her.

III.

Pour forth, mine eyes, the fountains of your tears,
Break, heart, and die, for now no hope appears.
Hope, upon which before my thoughts were fed,
Hath left me quite forlorn and from me fled.
Yet see, she smiles; O see, some hope appears.
Hold, heart, and live; mine eyes, cease off your tears.

IV.

Stay, nymph, the ground seeks but to kiss thy feet.
Hark, hark, how Philomela sweetly sings;
Whilst wanton wanton fishes, as they meet,
Strike crotchet-time amidst these crystal springs,
And Zephyrus 'mongst the leaves sweet murmur rings.
Stay but a while, Phoebe no tell-tale is,
She her Endymion, I'll my Phoebe kiss.

V.

Dorus, a seely shepherd swain
   Whilst he his flock was keeping
Upon the vast Arcadian plain,
   Found Amoretta sleeping.
And fearing lest she had been slain
   His eyes burst forth a-weeping.
Yet feeling her pure pulses beat,
   Not minding to molest her,
He viewed her most admired parts,
   And so most kindly kissed her.

VI.

Is this thy doom, and shall thy shepherd die,
Wounded with love, stabbed with affection's eye?
Say then, sweet saint, what breast shall be thy shrine
When thou hast slain the heart that erst was thine?
Pity, O pity, O life for love me give,
And sweetly say to me: Kind shepherd, live.

VII.

Amyntas with his fair Phyllis fair in height of Summer's sun
Grazed arm in arm their snowy flock; and scorching heat to shun
Under a spreading elm sat down, where love's delightments done,
Down dillie down, thus did they sing, there is no life like ours,
No heaven on earth to shepherds' cells, no hell to princely bowers.

VIII.

Here rest, my thoughts. What meaneth all this hasting
To fry in pangs and torments everlasting?
And yet her heart is e'en to me as cruel;
Her eye's the flame, but my heart lends the fuel.

IX.

Why should I grieve that she disdains my love,
   Or seek for love, since love's a grief?
A noble mind his tortures ill behove.
   He spoils, thralls, murders like a thief,
   Debarring beauty's bar all loved relief.

X.

The messenger of the delightful Spring,
    The cuckoo, proud bird mocking man,
On lofty oaks and every under-spring
    To chant out "cuckoo" scarce began,
    Whenas Menalcas, soote as swan
His Winter cloak cast off, did nimbly spring,
    And as the cuckoo "cuck" did sing,
The shepherd's down was Farra diddle dan.

XI.

Have I found her, (O rich finding!)
    Goddess-like for to behold,
Her fair tresses seemly binding
    In a chain of pearl and gold?
Chain me, chain me, O most fair,
Chain me to thee with that hair.

XII.

What though her frowns and hard entreaties kill
I will not cease to love, affect her still.
Still will I love her beauty, hate her scorn,
Love her for beauty at her beauty's morn.

XIII.

Love is a secret feeding fire that gives all creatures being,
Life to the dead, speech to the dumb, and to the blind man seeing.
And yet in me he contradicts all these his sacred graces,
Sears up my lips, my eyes, my life, and from me ever flying,
Leads me in paths untracked, ungone, and many uncouth places,
Where in despair I beauty curse, curse love and all fair faces.

XIV.

    Why do I fret and grieve
Since she denies and will no comfort give?
    O fatal foul decree.
She stops her ears and smiles at my complaint;
    Whilst, wounded with disdain,
I seek all means I can to set me free.
    And yet it will not be.
        O bitter pain!

XV.

All in a cave a shepherd's lad met wanton Thestalis,
Where he, unskilled in better sports, begged only for a kiss.
Alas, quoth she, and take thee this, and this, and this, and this;
But know'st thou not, fair boy, in love a more contented sweet?
O no, he said, for in a kiss our souls together meet.

XVI.

Sing we, dance we, on the green
And fill these valleys with melodious strains,
For joy that our Summer's queen,
Environed with all the country swains,
Fairly trips it o'er the plains.
Let us about these daffadillies sweet
Tread a ring-dance with our feet.

XVII.

Under the tops of Helicon
Not far from Parnass' stately towers
Springs forth the fountain Hippocrene
With banks beset with fragrant flowers.
The hill is it my Muses use,
The fountain which my heart doth choose.

XVIII.

Sweet Phillida, my flocks as white and pure as snowy down
Sit mourning for thy sake.
Come when thou wilt, I never mean to frown.
Thy love I will partake.
Come, quickly come, I sigh for thee my sweet.
I'll turn my flocks away,
And with them I'll not stay,
So thee and I most lovingly in love each other meet.

XIX.

My heart is dead within me,
For that my love forsakes me.
Yet why should I shed tears in vain?
She will not once respect my pain.
I'll therefore joy, and sing, and dance
In hope to cast a better chance.

XX.

No, no, no, it will not be,
Your labour is in vain.
I stay you not, but set you free;
Why do you then complain
And wail conceited wrongs as done to me?
No, no, I tell you once again
You have your travail for your pain.

XXI.

When Oriana walked to take the air
The world did strive to entertain so fair,
By Flora fair the sweetest flowers were strewn
Along the way for her to tread upon.
The trees did blossom, silver rivers ran,
The wind did gently play upon her fan.
And then for to delight her Grace's ear,
The woods a temple seemed, the birds a choir.
Then sang the shepherds and nymphs of Diana:
In heaven lives Oriana.

XXII.

Now I see thou floutest me,
And disdains the gifts I offer thee.
Then since thou scorns t' accept it
On Cloris' head I'll set it.
For her I'll gather dainty posies
Of gilliflowers and purple roses.
With her on each holiday
I'll dance the merry roundelay.
And this I know will move thee,
To say: I do not love thee.

NOTES

IV.—This is the second stanza of a poem which Pilkington set in full in his book of Airs, or lute-songs. In his other version he has *Fear not* for *stay*, *nymph* in line 1; and in line 3 for *wanton wanton* the lute-song version reads *water-wanton*. The first stanza was also set by Bateson.

X.—Line 3. *Under-spring:* sc. *undergrowth.*
Line 5. *soote:* sc. *sweet*, *gentle.*

XI.—Also set as a madrigal by Bateson, Pilkington's colleague at Chester Cathedral.

XXI.—The third example in the set of words also used by Bateson.

THE
FIRST SET
OF
MADRIGALS
AND PASTORALS
of 3. 4. and 5. Parts.

NEWLY COMPOSED

by FRANCIS PILKINGTON, Bat-
chelor of Muſicke and Luteniſt, and one of
the Cathedrall Church of Chriſt and
bleſſed *Mary* the Virgin
in *Cheſter.*

LONDON:
Printed for *M. L.*, *I. B.* and *T. S.*
the Aſſignes of *W. Barley.*

1613

TO THE RIGHT WOR^shipfull,

Sir *Thomas Smith* of Hough, in the Countie of Cheſter, Knight; *Francis Pilkington* Batchelor of Muſicke, and Luteniſt, wiſheth all happines in this *life, and eternall felicity in the life to come.*

Right Worſhipfull, there is held an infallible opinion, that the ſacred Art of *Muſicke* (being chiefly illuſtrated by Voyces) notwithſtanding all Artiſts, in reſpect of the compaſſe and quality of voyces and inſtruments, doe limit it within ſcales and other certaine dimenſions, is in its owne nature INFINITE; reaching from the baſe Earth (being as it were the GAM-VT or ground) to the higheſt E.LA. of the incomprehenſible heauens: For demonſtration whereof, GOD to his great Glory, doth diuerſly and wonderfully enable his creatures thereunto, teaching man vpon earth, not onely in mellifluous Notes to chant; but alſo vpon variety of Inſtruments ſweetly to expreſſe the hidden ſecrets of that ſacred Science, & not leauing the vaſt Ayre empty of his glory; he inſtructeth the early Larke to warble forth his prayſe; who, (as ſome hould) learneth his layes from the muſicall motions of the heauenly Spheares, and from thence to tranſcend vp to the ſeate of the moſt higheſt, the elected Saints and Angels doe in heauenly Himmes, ſing perpetually *Te deum* to the holy Trinitie, ſitting on the Throne of moſt Maieſticke glorie.

In which quality of Muſicke (Right worſhipfull) hauing ſpent a great part of my time, I haue now (after ſome others) of late produced this ſmall peece of worke; which albeit for the inſufficiency thereof, I doe hold to be too vnworthie to be preſented to your Worship, yet in regarde of the many and manifold fauors, which I haue receiued at your hands, and your exquiſit skill, both in the Theorique and Practique of that excellent Art; I doe preſume to tender it to your Patronage and protection, chuſing rather to be cenſured for ouer-boldneſſe, then to be taxed with ingratitude or forgetfulneſſe. And ſo humbly deſiring your Worſhip to accept of this, and to ſhield it from all pragmaticall and ſtigmaticall detractors; vntill my beſt ſkill and endeauour, ſhall incite my weake Muſe to performe ſome worke of better worth, I craue pardon for my bouldneſſe, and commit your Worſhip and the good Lady your wife, to the bleſſed tuition of the God of Iſraell.

From my manſion in the Monaſtery of Cheſter
the 25. *day of September* 1612.

Your worſhips in all obſeruancy

Francis Pilkington.

TABLE OF CONTENTS

Francis Pilkington's

First Set of Madrigals.

(1613)

Edited by EDMUND H. FELLOWES.
Revised by THURSTON DART.

No 1. SEE WHERE MY LOVE.

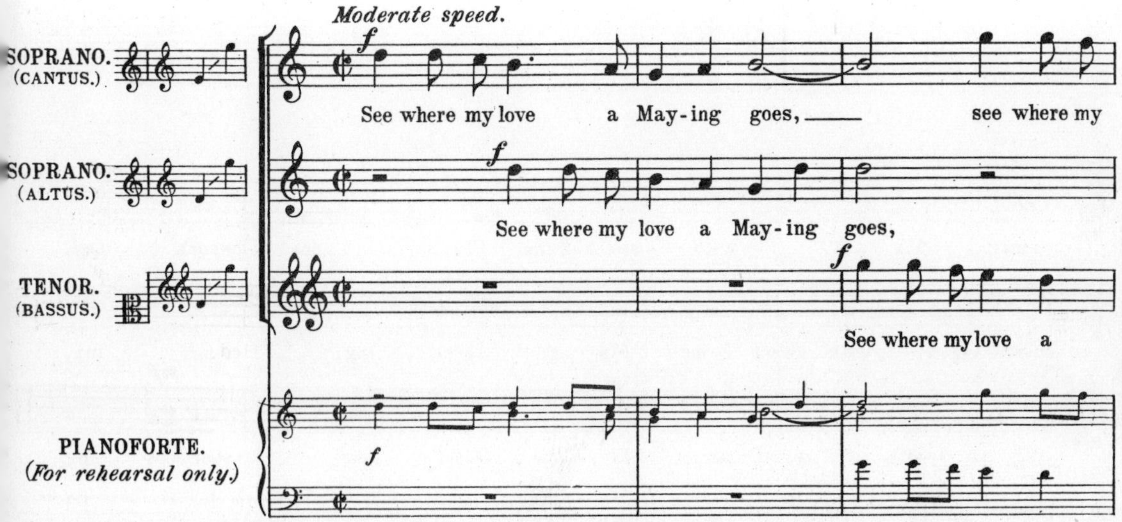

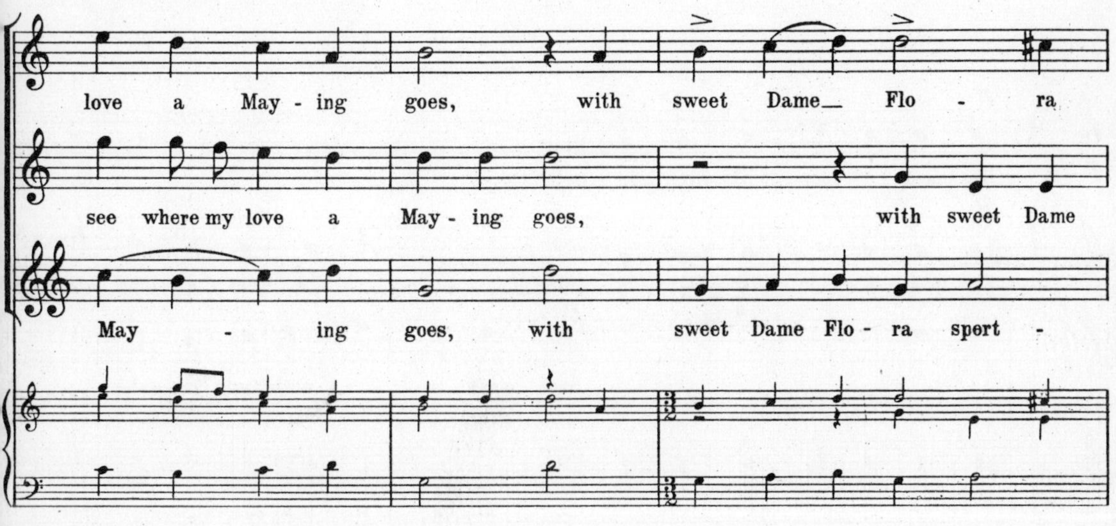

sport-ing, with sweet Dame Flo-ra sport - ing, with sweet Dame Flo - ra
Flo - ra sport-ing, with sweet Dame Flo - ra sport-ing, with sweet Dame Flo-ra
- ing, with sweet Dame Flo - ra sport - ing, with sweet Dame Flo - ra sport -
sport - ing, with sweet Dame Flo - ra sport - ing,
sport-ing, with sweet Dame Flo - ra sport - ing, sport - ing,
- ing, with sweet Dame Flo - ra sport - ing, sport - ing,
p
She most a - lone with Night - in - gales, she
p
She most a - lone with Night - in - gales, she most a - lone with
p
She most a - lone with Night - in - gales,
p

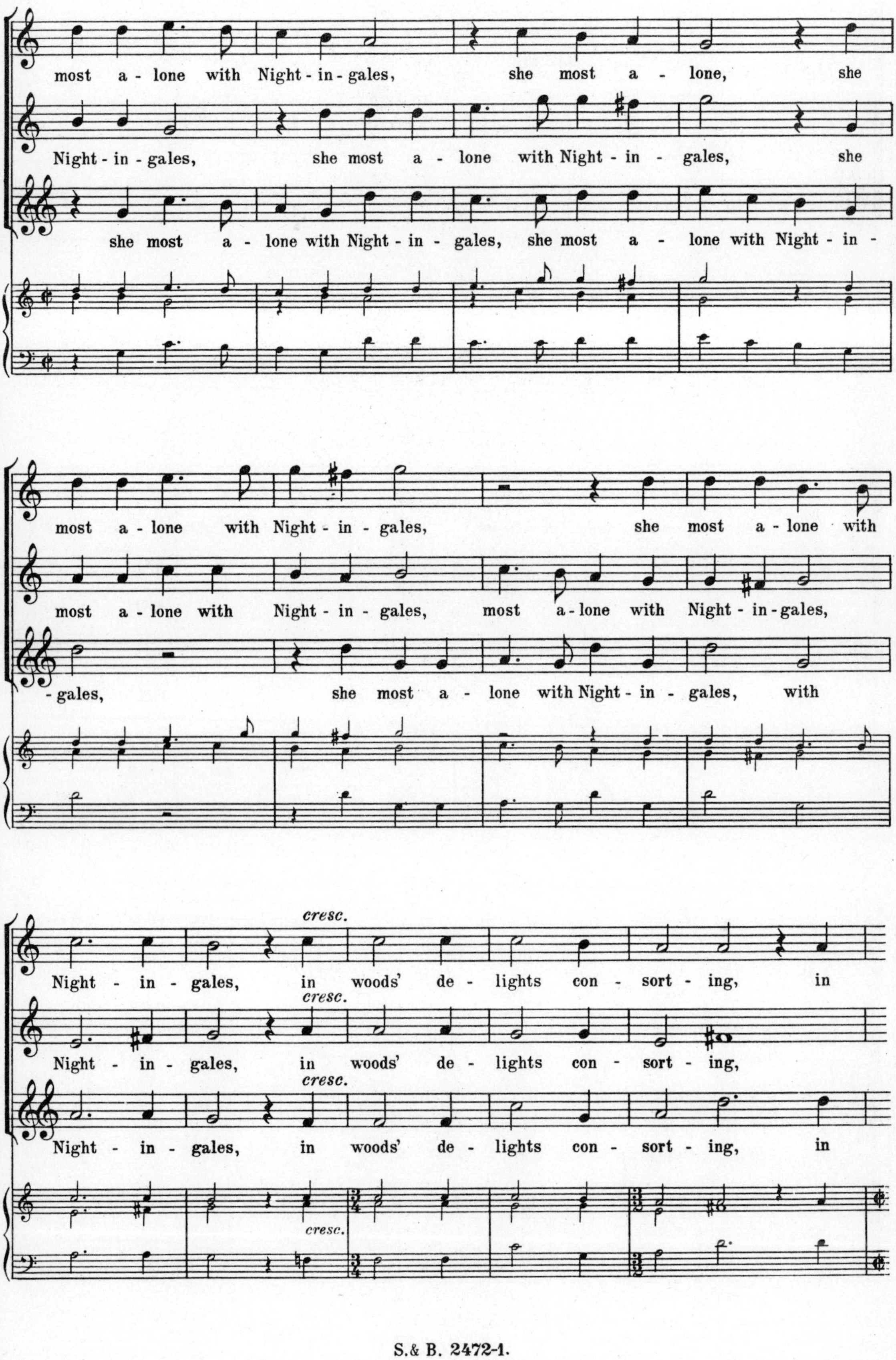
most a - lone with Night - in - gales, she most a - lone, she
Night - in - gales, she most a - lone with Night - in - gales, she
she most a - lone with Night - in - gales, she most a - lone with Night - in -
most a - lone with Night - in - gales, she most a - lone with
most a - lone with Night - in - gales, most a - lone with Night - in - gales,
- gales, she most a - lone with Night - in - gales, with
cresc.
Night - in - gales, in woods' de - lights con - sort - ing, in
cresc.
Night - in - gales, in woods' de - lights con - sort - ing,
cresc.
Night - in - gales, in woods' de - lights con - sort - ing, in
cresc.

mf
woods' de - lights con - sort - ing, in woods' de - lights con -
in woods' de - lights, in woods' de - - lights
woods' de - lights con - sort - ing, in woods' de - - lights con -
- sort - ing, in woods' de - lights, in woods' de - lights con - sort -
con - sort - ing, in woods' de - lights con - sort -
- sort - ing, in woods' de - lights con - sort - ing,
f
- ing, in woods' de - lights con - - - -
- ing, in woods' de - - lights con -
in woods' de - lights con - sort -

p
sort - - ing. Turn a - - - - gain, turn a-
sort - ing. Turn a - gain, turn a-
- - ing. Turn a - - - - gain, turn a-
- - - gain, turn a - gain my
- - gain, turn a - gain my
- - gain, turn a - gain my
cresc.
mf
dear - est, The pleas - ant'st air's in mea-dows, the pleasant'st air's in
dear - est, The pleas - ant'st air's in mea-dows, the pleas-ant'st
dear - est, The pleas - ant'st air's in mea-dows, the pleas - ant'st

p
mf
mea - dows, the pleas - ant'st air's in mea - dows,
air's in mea - dows, the pleas - ant'st air's in mea - dows,
air's in mea - dows, the pleas - ant'st
the pleas - ant'st air's in mea-dows, Else by the ri - vers let us
the pleas - ant'st air's in mea-dows, Else by the ri - vers
air's in mea-dows, Else by the ri - vers
breathe, else by the ri - vers let us breathe, else
let us breathe, else by the ri - vers let us breathe,
let us breathe, else by the ri - vers let us breathe,

mf
p
by the ri - vers let us breathe, else by the ri - vers let us
else by the ri - vers let us breathe, let us
else by the ri - vers let us
breathe, and kiss, and kiss, and kiss, and
breathe, and kiss, and kiss, and kiss, and
breathe, and kiss, and kiss, and kiss, and
kiss a - mongst the wil - - lows.
kiss a - mongst the wil - lows, the wil - - lows.
kiss a - mongst the wil - - lows.

Nº 2. I FOLLOW, LO, THE FOOTING.

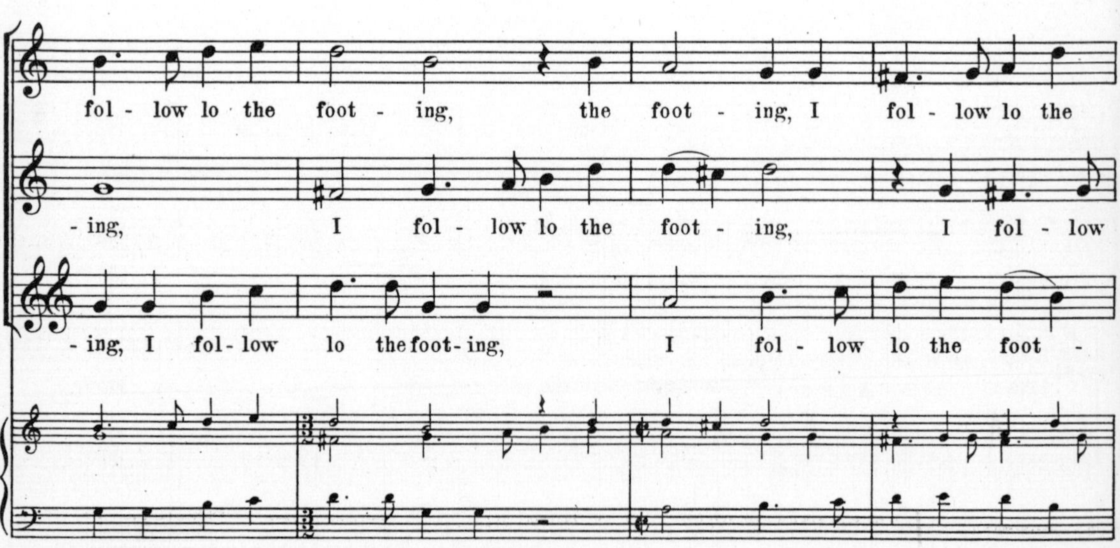

foot - ing, I fol-low lo the foot-ing still of my
lo the foot-ing, I fol - low lo the foot-ing still of my
-ing, I fol - low lo the foot - ing still of my
f
love - ly cru - el. Proud of her-self, proud of her-self,
f
love - ly cru - el. Proud of her - self, proud of her-self, proud of her -
f
love - ly cru - el. Proud of her-self, proud of her-self,
f
proud of her-self, that she is beau - ty's jew -
-self, proud of her - self that she is beau - ty's jew -
proud of her-self, her - self that she is beau - ty's jew -

p
-el, And fast a-way she fli-eth, And
p
-el, And fast a-way she fli-eth, and fast a-way she fli-
p
-el, And fast a-way she fli-eth,
p
cresc.
fast a-way she fli-eth, and fast a-way she fli-eth,
cresc.
-eth, and fast a-way she fli-eth, and fast a-way she fli-eth,
cresc.
and fast a-way she fli-eth, and fast a-way she fli-eth,
cresc.
mf
p
Love's sweet de-light de-rid-ing, In woods and
mf
p
Love's sweet de-light de-rid-ing, In woods and groves, in
mf
p
Love's sweet de-light de-rid-ing, In woods and
mf
p

mf
groves, in woods and groves sweet Na-ture's trea-sure hid - ing. Yet
woods and groves, in woods and groves sweet Na-ture's trea-sure hid - ing. Yet
groves, in woods and___ groves sweet Na-ture's trea-sure hid - ing. Yet
cease I not pur - su - ing, yet cease I not pur - su - ing, yet
cease I not pur - su - ing, yet cease I not pur -
cease I not pur - su - ing, yet cease I not pur - su - ing, yet
f
cease I not pur - su - ing, yet cease I not pur - su - ing, But
- su - ing, yet cease I not pur - su - ing, pur - su - ing,
cease I not pur - su - ing, yet cease I not pur - su - ing,

since I thus have sought her I thus have sought her, Will run me out of
f
But since I thus have sought her, Will run me out of
f
But since I thus have sought her,
breath, will run me out of breath, will run me out of breath
breath, will run me out of breath, will
Will run me out of breath, will run me out of breath, will
1.
2.
mf
Till I have caught her. Yet her.
mf
run me out of breath Till I have caught her. Yet her.
mf
run me out of breath Till I have caught her. Yet her.
mf

Nº 3. POUR FORTH, MINE EYES.

mf
eyes the foun - tains of your tears, Break heart, break heart, and—
mf
eyes the foun - tains of your tears, Break heart, break
mf
eyes the foun - tains of your tears, Break heart, break heart, and die,
mf
dim.
die, break heart, break heart, and die, break heart, and
dim.
heart, and die, break heart, break heart, and— die, break
dim.
break heart, break heart, and die, break heart, break heart, and
dim.
p
mf
die, and die, for now no hope ap - pears, Hope up - on which, hope up - on
p
mf
heart, and die, for now no hope ap - pears, Hope up - on which, hope up -
p
mf
die, for now no hope ap - pears, Hope up - on which,
p
mf

which, up - on — which, up - on which, up - on
-on which, hope up - on which, up - on
hope up - on which, — hope up - on which,
which be - fore my thoughts were fed,
which be - fore my thoughts were fed, Hath left me
up - on which be - fore my thoughts were fed, Hath
p
p
p
Hath left me quite for - lorn, quite for - lorn, hath
quite for - - lorn, hath left me quite for - lorn, hath
left me quite for - lorn, hath left me quite for - lorn,
p

*In the repeated section this is misprinted E.

see, O see some hope ap - pears, O see some hope ap -
see some hope ap - pears, O see some hope ap - pears, ap -
see some hope ap - pears, O see some hope, some hope ap -
-pears. Hold heart and live, hold heart and live, hold
-pears. Hold heart and live, hold heart and
-pears. Hold heart and live, and
heart and live, Mine eyes cease off your tears. Yet tears.
live, Mine eyes cease off your tears. Yet tears.
live, Mine eyes cease off your tears. Yet tears.

Nº 4. STAY, NYMPH, O STAY.

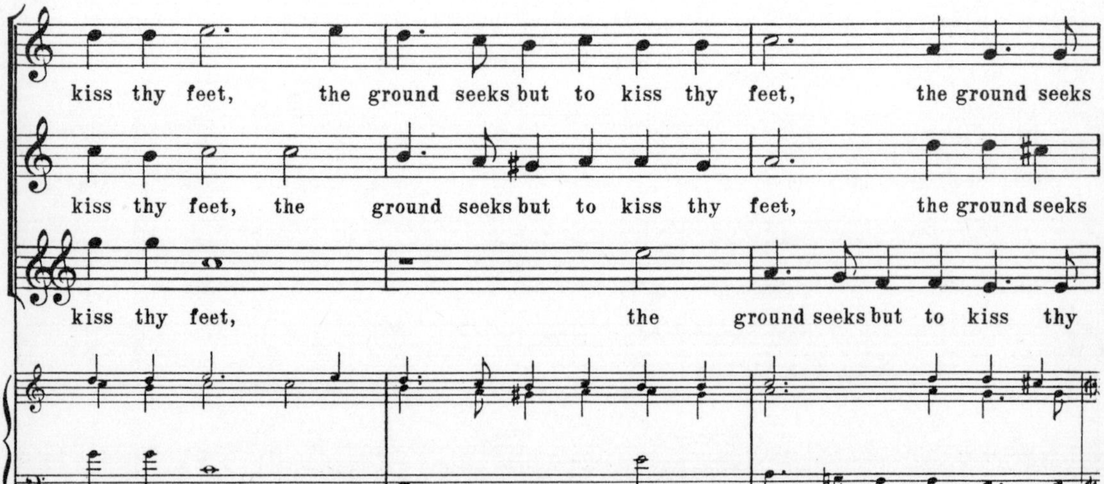

f
p
but to kiss thy feet. Hark, hark, hark how
but to kiss thy feet. Hark, hark, hark how
feet. Hark, hark, hark how
Phi-lo-me-la sweet-ly sings, how Phi - lo-me-la, how
Phi-lo-me-la sweet-ly sings, how Phi-lo-me-la, how Phi - lo-
Phi-lo-me-la sweet-ly sings, how Phi - lo-me-la,
mf
Phi - lo-me-la, how Phi - lo - me - - la sweet-ly sings, Whilst
-me-la, how Phi - lo-me-la sweet-ly, sweet - ly sings, Whilst
how Phi - lo-me-la, how Phi - lo-me-la sweet-ly sings,

* Bateson's setting reads water-wanton.
† E D C in original

meet, strike crot - chet, crot - chet time, strike
strike crot - chet, crot - chet time, strike crot - chet, crot - chet
meet, strike crot - chet, crot - chet time, strike crot - chet
crot - chet, crot - chet time, strike crot - chet, crot - chet time a -
time, strike crot - chet, crot - chet time, crot - chet time a -
crot - chet time, strike crot - chet, crot - chet time a - -
-midst the crys-tal springs, And Ze - phy-rus 'mongst the leaves, the
-midst the crys-tal springs, And Ze - phy-rus 'mongst the leaves sweet
-midst the crys-tal springs, And Ze - phy-rus 'mongst the leaves sweet mur - mur-

leaves sweet mur - mur rings, sweet mur - mur
mur - mur rings, sweet mur-mur
rings, sweet mur - mur rings, sweet mur - mur rings,
rings, sweet mur - mur rings, sweet mur - - mur
rings, sweet mur - mur rings, sweet mur - - - mur
sweet mur - mur rings, sweet mur - mur, mur - mur
mf
rings. Stay but a - while, stay but a - while, stay but a - while
rings. Stay but a - while, stay but a - while Phoe -
rings. Stay but a-while, stay but a-while, Phoe - be no

Phoe - be no tell - tale is, She her En-dy-mi-on,
- be no tell-tale is, no tell-tale is, She her En-dy-mi-on,
tell-tale, Phoe - be no tell-tale is, She
her En-dy-mi-on, I'll my Phoe - be kiss,
her En-dy-mi-on, I'll my Phoe - be kiss,
her En-dy-mi-on, I'll my Phoe - be kiss,
I'll my Phoe - be kiss, I'll my Phoe - be kiss.
I'll my Phoe - be___ kiss, I'll my Phoe - be___ kiss.
I'll my Phoe - be kiss, I'll my Phoe - be kiss.
cresc.

Nº 5. DORUS, A SEELY SHEPHERD.

he his flock was keep - ing Up - on the vast, up - on the
he his flock was keep - ing Up - on the vast Ar - ca - dian
he his flock was keep - ing Up - on the
vast Ar - ca - di - an plain, found A - mo - ret - ta
plain, Ar - ca - di - an plain, found A - mo - ret - ta
vast Ar - ca - di - an plain, found A - mo - ret - ta
p
sleep - ing, And fear - ing lest she had been slain, and
cresc.
sleep - ing, A - mo - ret - ta sleep - ing, And fear - ing lest she
sleep - ing, And fear - ing lest she had been slain,

cresc.
mf
fear - ing lest she had been slain, and fear - ing lest she
had been slain, and fear - ing lest she had been slain,
and fear - ing lest she had been slain, she
p
had been slain, and fear - ing lest she had been slain,
and fear - ing lest she had been slain, and fear - ing lest
had been slain, and fear - ing lest she had been slain, lest
she had been slain, his eyes burst forth a
she had been slain, his eyes burst forth a weep -
she had been slain, his eyes burst forth a

p
weep - ing, his eyes burst forth a
p
- ing, his eyes burst forth a weep - ing, a
p
weep - ing, his eyes burst forth a weep - ing,
p
mf
dim.
weep - ing, his eyes burst forth a weep - - -
mf
dim.
weep - ing, his eyes burst forth a weep - ing,
mf
dim.
his eyes burst forth a weep -
mf
dim.
p
- ing, Yet feel - ing her pure pul - ses
p
Yet feel - ing her pure pul - ses beat, yet
p
- ing, Yet feel - ing her pure pul - ses beat,
p

beat, her pure pul - ses beat, her pure pul - ses beat, her pure
feel - ing her pure pul - ses beat, yet feel - ing her pure
yet feel - ing her pure pul - ses beat, her pure
pp
pul - ses beat, not mind - ing to mo - lest her, not mind - ing to mo -
pp
pul - ses beat, not mind - ing to mo - lest her, not mind - ing to mo -
pp
pul - ses beat, not mind - ing to mo - lest her, not mind - ing to mo -
pp
mf
- lest her, He viewed her most ad - mir - ed parts,
mf
- lest her, He viewed her most ad - mir - ed,
mf
- lest her, He viewed her most ad - mir - ed parts, he viewed her most ad -
mf

he viewed her most ad-mir - ed parts, he viewed her most ad-
-mir - ed parts, he viewed her most ad-mir - ed parts, he viewed her most ad-
-mir - ed parts, he viewed her most ad-mir - ed
-mir - ed parts, he viewed her most ad-mir - ed
-mir - ed parts, he viewed her most ad-mir - ed parts, he
parts, he viewed her most ad-mir - ed parts, he
p
parts, ad - mir - ed parts, and so most kind - ly kissed her.
viewed her most ad-mir - ed parts, and so most kind-ly, kind - ly kissed her.
viewed her most ad-mir - ed parts, and so most kind - ly kissed her.

Nº 6. IS THIS THY DOOM?

mf
shep - herd die? Wound - ed with Love, wound - ed with
mf
and shall thy shep - herd die? Wound - ed with Love, wound -
mf
shep - herd die? Wound - ed with Love,
mf
dim.
Love, wound - ed with Love, wound-ed with
dim.
- ed, wound-ed with Love, wound-ed with Love,
dim.
wound - ed, wound-ed with Love, wound -
dim.
p
mf
Love, wound-ed with Love, stabbed with af - fec - tion's
p
mf
wound - ed with Love, stabbed with af - fec - tion's
p
- ed with Love,
p
mf

f
eye, stabbed with af - fec - tion's eye,
f
eye, stabbed with af - fec - tion's eye,
f
mf
stabbed with af - fec - tion's eye, Say then sweet
f
mf
mf
Say then sweet Saint, say then sweet
mf
Say then sweet Saint, say then sweet Saint, say then sweet
Saint, say then sweet Saint, say then sweet
Saint, what breast shall be thy shrine, thy
Saint, what breast shall be thy
Saint, what breast shall be thy shrine, thy

p
shrine? When thou hast slain the heart, when
shrine? When thou hast slain the heart, when
shrine? When thou hast slain the heart, when thou hast slain the
thou hast slain the heart, hast slain the heart, that erst was
thou hast slain the heart, hast slain the
heart, when thou hast slain the heart,
mf
thine, when thou hast slain the heart that erst was thine,
heart, when thou hast slain the heart that erst was thine,
when thou hast slain the heart that erst was thine,

p
mf
Pi - ty, O pi - ty, pi - ty, O
Pi - ty, O pi - ty, pi - ty, O pi - ty,
Pi - ty, O pi - ty, pi - ty, O pi - ty,
pi - ty, O pi - ty, O life for love me
pi - ty, O pi - ty, O life for love me
pi - ty, O pi - ty, O life for love me
give, And sweet - ly say to me, and sweet -
give, And sweet - ly say to
give, And sweet - ly say,

Heere endeth the three Parts.

Nº 7. AMYNTAS WITH HIS PHYLLIS FAIR.

with his Phyl-lis fair, in height of sum-mer's Sun, in height of
-mer's Sun, of sum-mer's Sun, in height of sum-mer's
sum-mer's Sun, in height of sum-mer's Sun, in
f
in height of sum-mer's Sun, in height of sum-mer's
sum-mer's Sun, in height of sum-mers Sun
Sun, in height of sum-mers Sun
height of sum-mer's Sun, of sum-mer's Sun
Sun, in height of sum-mer's Sun
mf
Grazed arm in arm,
grazed arm in arm their snow-y flock,
grazed arm in arm their snow-y flock, and scorch-ing heat to
grazed arm in arm their snow-y flock, and scorch-ing heat to
grazed arm in arm their snow-y flock,

dim.
and scorch - ing heat, scorch - ing heat to
dim.
shun, and scorch - ing heat to shun,
dim.
shun, and scorch - ing heat to
dim.
and scorch - ing heat to shun, to
dim.
p
shun, Un - der a spread - ing Elm sat
p
Un - der a spread - ing Elm sat down, Where love's de - light - ments
p
shun, Un - der a spread - ing Elm sat down,
p
shun, Un - der a spread - ing Elm sat down, un - der a spread - ing
p
cresc.
down, un - der a spread - ing Elm sat down,
cresc.
done, where
cresc.
un - der a spread - ing Elm sat down, Where love's de -
Elm sat down, Where love's de - light - ments done,
cresc.

Where love's de - light - ments done,
love's de - light - ments done, where love's de - light - ments done,
- light - ments done, where love's de - light - ments done,
where love's de - light - ments done, de - light - ments done,
Down, down, down, down, down, down, dil - lie down, down, down, down,
Down, down, down, down, down, down, dil - lie down,
Down, down,
Down, down, down, dil - lie down, down, down,
down, dil - lie down, Thus did they sing, There
Thus did they sing, There
down, dil - lie down, Thus did they sing, There
down, dil - lie down, Thus did they sing, There

f
is no life like ours, no life like ours, No heaven on
is no life like ours, no life like ours,
is no life like ours, no life like ours,
is no life like ours, no life like ours, No
earth to shep - herds' Cells, to shep-herds' Cells, to shep-herds' Cells,
No heaven on earth to shep - herds' Cells,
No heaven on earth to shep - herds' Cells,
heaven on earth, no heaven on earth to shep-herds' Cells,
No hell to Prince - ly Bowers. Bowers.
No hell to Prince - - ly Bowers. Bowers.
No hell to Prince - - - ly Bowers. Bowers.
No hell to Prince - ly Bowers. Bowers.
1
2

Nº 8. HERE REST, MY THOUGHTS.

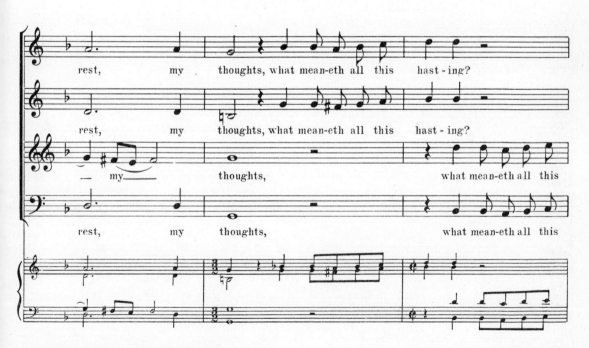

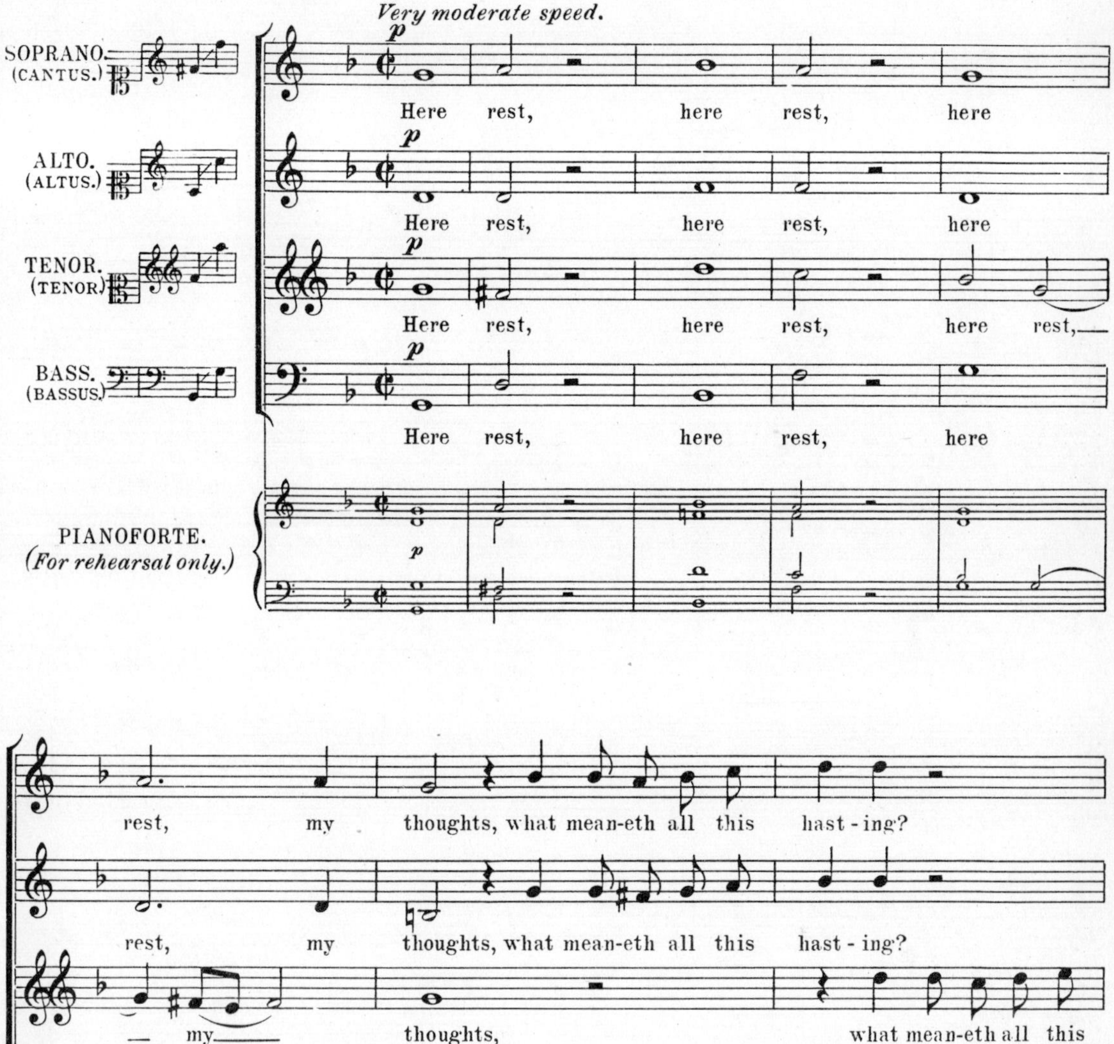

cresc.
what mean - eth all this hast - ing, hast - - -
cresc.
what mean - eth all this hast - ing?
hast - ing?
cresc.
what mean - eth all this
hast - ing?
cresc.
what mean - eth all this
cresc.
mf
- ing? what mean-eth all this hast - ing? what mean - eth all this
mf
what mean-eth all this hast - ing? what mean-eth all this hast -
hast - ing?
mf
what mean-eth all this hast - - -
hast - ing?
mf
what mean-eth all this hast - ing, all this
mf
f
hast-ing? To fry in pangs and tor-ments, to
f
- ing, hast - ing? To fry in pangs and tor -
f
- ing? To fry in pangs, to fry in pangs and
f
hast - ing? To fry in pangs and tor -
f

fry in pangs and tor-ments ev-er-last - ing, ev-er -
-ments, to fry in pangs and tor-ments ev-er -
tor-ments, in pangs and tor-ments, and tor-ments ev - er -
-ments, to fry in pangs and tor-ments ev - er -
-last - ing. And yet her heart is ev-en to me as
-last - ing. And yet her heart is ev-en to me as
-last - ing. And yet her heart is ev-en to me as
-last - ing. And yet her heart is ev-en to me as
cru-el, is even to me as cru - el, Her eye's the
cru-el, is even to me as cru-el, Her eye's
cru-el, is even to me as cru - el, Her eye's the
cru-el, is even to me as cru - el, Her eye's

*misprinted as A.

but my heart lends the fu - el,
but my heart lends the fu - el, but my heart lends the
but my heart lends the fu - el, but my heart lends the
my heart lends the fu - el, but my
cresc.
but my heart lends the fu - el, but my
fu - el, but my heart lends the fu - el, but my
fu - el, but my heart
heart lends the
f
p
1.
2.
heart lends the fu - el. And - el.
heart lends the fu - el. And - el.
lends the fu - el. And - el.
fu - el. And - el.

Nº 9. WHY SHOULD I GRIEVE?

should I grieve,
p
why should I grieve, why
I grieve, why should I grieve,
I grieve, why should I grieve, why
cresc.
why should I grieve, why should I
should I grieve, why should I grieve, why
why should I grieve, why should I grieve that
should I grieve, why should I grieve, why
mf
grieve that she dis-dains, dis-dains my
should I grieve that she dis-dains my
she dis-dains my love? that she dis - dains my
should I grieve that she dis - dains my

p
love? Or seek for love,
mf
or
p
love? Or seek for love,
or seek for love,
love,
p
love?
Or seek for love,
or seek for
p
love? Or seek for love,
or
seek for love,
or seek for
p
p
seek for love,
or seek for love,
p
or seek for love since
mf
p
or seek for love,
or seek for love,
or seek for
love,
mf
or seek for love,
or seek for love,
love,
mf
or seek for love
p
since love's a
mf
p
love's a grief? since love, since love's a grief,
since
love
since love's a grief,
since
p
since love's a grief, since love's a grief,
since
grief?
love's a grief,
since

mf
love's a grief? A no - ble mind, a
love's a grief? A no - ble mind, a no - ble mind,
love's a grief? A no - ble mind, a no - ble mind, a
love's a grief? A no - ble mind, a no - ble mind, a
cresc.
no - ble mind, a no - ble mind his
a no - ble, no - ble mind, a
no - ble mind, a no - ble, no - ble mind, a no - ble
no - ble mind, a no - ble mind, a no - ble mind
f
tor - tures ill be - hove, his tor - tures ill be - hove.
no - ble mind his tor - tures ill be - hove. He
mind his tor - tures ill be - hove.
his tor - tures ill be - hove, his tor - tures ill be - hove.

He spoils, thralls, murd-ers like a
— spoils, thralls, — murd - ers — like a — thief, like
He spoils, thralls, — murd-ers, he spoils, thralls, —
He — spoils, thralls, — murd - ers like a
thief, he spoils, thralls, — murd - ers like a thief,
a thief, he — spoils, thralls, murd - ers
— murd-ers, he spoils, thralls, murd - ers
thief, he — spoils, thralls, — murd - ers like a thief,
mf
like a — thief, De - bar - ring beau - ty's —
like a thief,
like a thief, De - bar - ring
like a thief, De - bar - ring beau - ty's —
mf

bar, de - bar - ring beau - ty's
mf
De - bar - ring beau - ty's bar,
beau - ty's, beau - ty's bar, beau - ty's bar, de -
bar, de - bar - ring beau - ty's bar,
dim.
bar all loved re - lief,
dim.
de - bar - ring beau - ty's bar all loved,
dim.
-bar - ring beau ty's bar all loved re - lief,
dim.
de - bar - ring beau - ty's bar all loved,
dim.
1.
2.
p
all loved re - - lief. - lief.
p
f
all loved re - lief, loved re - lief. He - lief.
p
all loved re - - lief. - lief.
p
all loved re - - lief. - lief.
p
f

Nº 10. THE MESSENGER OF SPRING.

On lof - ty Oaks and ev - ery un - der-
ev - ery un-der - spring, and ev - ery un - der-spring, and ev - ery un - der-
ev - ery un-der - spring, and ev - ery un - der-spring, and ev - ery un - der-
On lof - ty Oaks and ev - ery un - der-
p
-spring to chant out cuc - koo cuc - koo scarce be - gan, to chant out
mf
-spring, and ev - ery un - der-spring to chant out cuc - koo cuc - koo
-spring, and ev - ery un - der-spring to chant out
-spring to chant out cuc - koo cuc - koo scarce be -
cuc-koo cuc-koo scarce be-gan, to chant out cuc-koo scarce be-gan, When-
scarce be-gan, to chant out cuc-koo cuc-koo scarce be - gan, When -
cuc-koo cuc-koo scarce be - gan, to chant out cuc - koo scarce be - gan, When-
-gan, to chant out cuc-koo cuc-koo scarce be - gan, When -

*Soote sc. sweet, or gentle.

cloak cast off, did nim-bly nim-bly spring, did
did nim-bly nim-bly spring, did spring, did
win - ter cloak cast off, did nim-bly nim-bly spring,
cloak cast off, did
nim - bly spring, did nim - bly spring, did nim-bly nim-bly spring, did
nim-bly nim-bly spring, did nim - bly spring, did nim-bly nim-bly nim - bly
did nim-bly nim-bly spring, did nim-bly nim-bly nim - bly
nim-bly nim-bly spring, did nim-bly nim-bly nim - bly
spring, And as the Cuc - koo, and as the Cuc - koo,
spring, And as the Cuc - koo, and as the
spring, And as the Cuc - koo, and as the
spring, And as the Cuc - koo,

p
and as the Cuc - koo, and as the Cuc - koo cuck did
Cuc - koo, and as the Cuc - koo, the Cuc - koo cuck did
Cuc - koo, Cuc - koo cuck did sing, Cuc - koo Cuc - koo cuck did
p
and as the Cuc - koo, and as the Cuc - koo cuck did
sing, The shep - herds' down, down a down a
sing, The shep - herds' down a down a down,
sing, The shep - herds' down, down a
sing, The shep - herds' down,
down, down a down a down, the shep-herds' down a down,
down a down a down, down a down, down a
down a down, down down a down, down a down down,
down a down a down, down a down a down, the shep-herds'

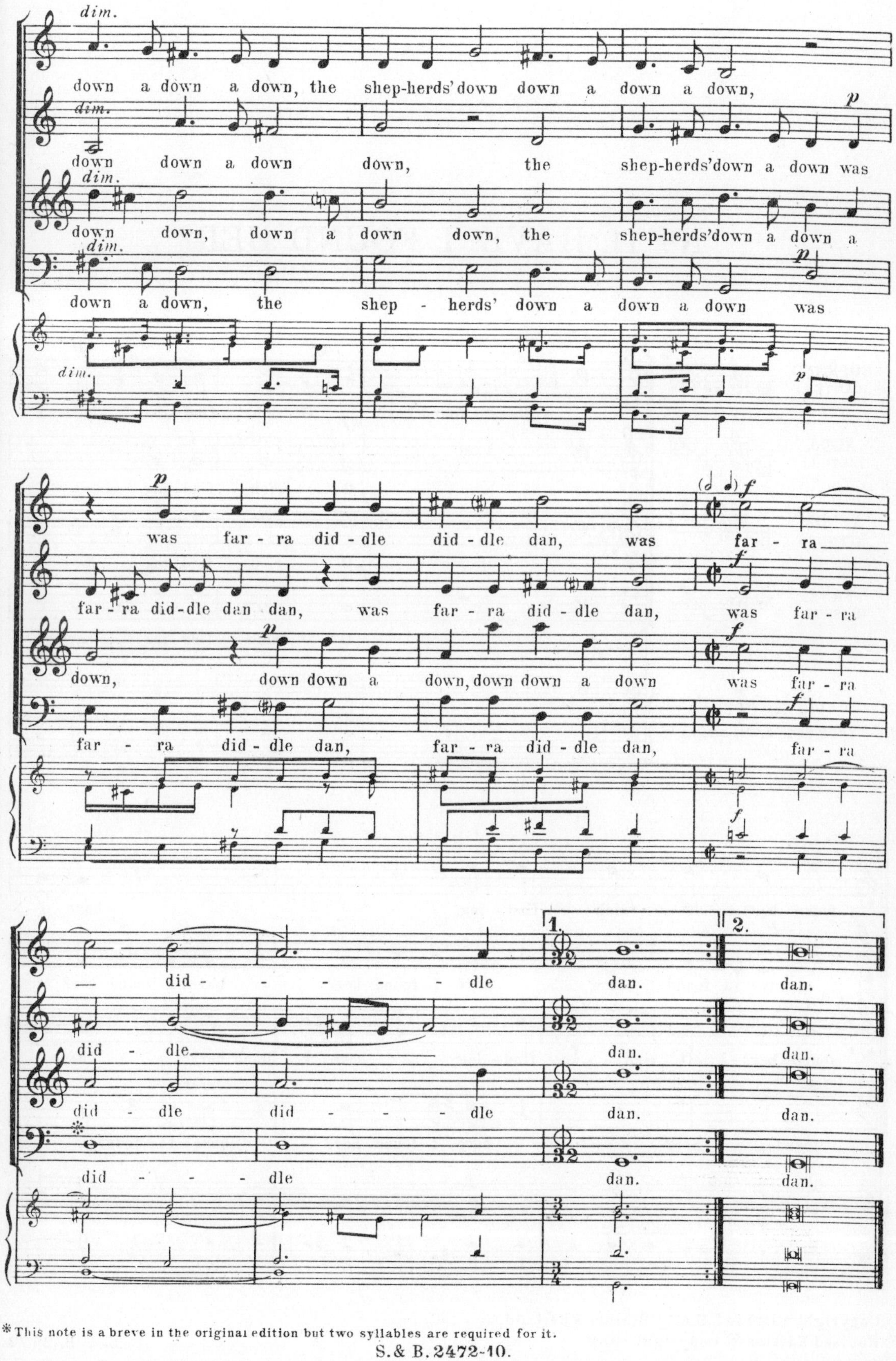

*This note is a breve in the original edition but two syllables are required for it.

Nº 11. HAVE I FOUND HER?

f
found her? O rich find - ing, O rich find -
O rich find - ing, O rich find -
I found her? O rich find -
her? have I found her? O rich find -
-ing, God-dess - like for to be - hold, God-dess -
-ing, God-dess - like for to be -
-ing, God-dess - like for to be - hold, for to be -
-ing, God-dess - like for to be - hold,
-like for to be - hold, God-dess - like for to
-hold, God-dess - like for to be - hold, for
-hold, God-dess - like for
God-dess - like for to be - hold, God-dess - like for

— be - hold, her fair tress - es —
to be - hold, for to be - hold,
to be - hold, to be - hold, her fair
to be - hold, her fair tress - es seem - ly
— seem - ly bind - ing, her
her fair — tress - es seem - ly
tress - es seem - ly bind - ing, seem - ly bind - -
bind - - ing, bind - - -
fair tress - es seem - ly bind - ing, her fair tress - es
bind - ing, seem - ly bind - ing, her fair tress - es
- ing, seem - ly bind - ing, her fair tress - es
- ing, her fair tress - es

seem - ly bind - ing In a chain of Pearl and
seem - ly bind - ing
seem - ly bind - ing In a chain of Pearl and
seem - ly bind - ing
Gold, in a chain of Pearl and Gold, in a
in a chain of Pearl and Gold,
Gold, of Pearl and Gold, in a chain of
in a chain of Pearl and Gold,
chain of Pearl and Gold, Pearl and Gold, in a chain of Pearl and
in a chain of Pearl and Gold, in a
Pearl and Gold, of Pearl and Gold, in a
in a chain of Pearl and Gold, in a chain of Pearl and Gold,

mf
Gold, in a chain of Gold, in a chain of
chain of Pearl and Gold, in a chain of Pearl, of
chain of Pearl and Gold, of
mf
in a chain of Pearl and Gold, of
(𝅗𝅥 = 𝅝.)
p repeat f
Pearl and Gold. Chain me, chain me, O most
Pearl and Gold. Chain me, chain me, O most
Pearl and Gold. Chain me, chain me, O most
Pearl and Gold. Chain me, chain me, O most
p repeat f
1.
2.
fair, Chain me to thee with that hair. hair.
fair, Chain me to thee with that hair. hair.
fair, Chain me to thee with that hair. hair.
fair, Chain me to thee with that hair. hair.

Nº 12. WHAT THOUGH HER FROWNS?

f
hard en-trea-ties kill? What though her
cresc.
hard en-trea-ties kill? What though her frowns
f
hard en-trea-ties kill? What though her frowns, what though her
f
What though her frowns, what though her
f
frowns and hard en - trea - ties kill? I will not cease to
f
and hard en - trea - ties kill?
frowns and hard en-trea - - ties kill?
frowns and hard en - trea - ties kill? I
love, I will not cease to
I will not cease to love, I will not cease to
I will not cease to love, I
will not cease to love, I will not cease to love,

love, I will not cease to love, I will not
love, I will not cease to love,
will not cease to love, I will not cease to love,
I will not cease to love, I will not
p
cease to love af - fect her, af - fect her still. Still will I love her
I will not cease to love af - fect her still.
cease to love af - fect her, af - fect her still. Still will I
cease to love af - fect her, af - fect her still. Still
p
beau - ty, still will I love her beau - ty,
Still will I love her beau - ty, still will I love her
love her beau - ty, still will I love her beau - ty,
will I love

cresc.
still will I love her beau - ty, still will I love her
cresc.
beau - ty, still will I love her beau - - - -
cresc.
still will I love her beau - ty, still will I love her
cresc.
her beau - - - - - - -
cresc.
f
beau - ty, hate her scorn, Love her for beau - ty, love her for
f
-ty, hate her scorn, Love her for beau - ty, love her for
f
beau - ty, hate her scorn, Love her for beau - ty, love her for
f
-ty, hate her scorn, Love her for beau - ty, love her for
f
p
beau - ty, at her beau - ty's morn, at her beau - - ty's
p
beau - ty, at her beau - ty's morn, at her beau - ty's
beau - ty,
beau - ty,
p

* This sharp is given to the previous note in the original edition in both places.

Nº 13. LOVE IS A SECRET FEEDING FIRE.

se - cret feed - ing fire, Love is a se - cret feed - ing
se - cret feed - ing fire, a se - cret feed - ing
fire, a se - cret feed - ing fire, a se - cret feed - ing
Love is a se - cret feed - ing fire,
cresc.
fire, that gives all crea - tures be - ing, that gives all
fire, that gives all crea - tures be - ing, that gives all
fire, that gives all crea - tures be - ing, that gives all
that gives all crea - tures be - ing, that gives all
crea - tures be - ing, Life to the dead, life to the dead,
crea - tures be - ing, Life to the dead, life to the dead,
crea - tures be - ing, Life to the dead, life to the
crea - tures be - ing, Life to the dead, life to the

life to the dead, speech to the
life to the dead, speech to the dumb, the
dead, life to the dead, speech to the
dead, life to the dead, speech to the
dumb, and to the blind man see - ing.
dumb, and to the blind man see - ing.
dumb, and to the blind man see - ing.
dumb, and to the blind man see - ing.
1.
2.
see - ing. And yet in me he con - tra - dicts,
see - ing. And yet in me he
see - ing. And yet in me he con -
see - ing. And yet in me in
p
p
p
p
p

he con - tra - dicts, he con - tra - dicts
con - tra-dicts, he con - tra-dicts, he
-tra - dicts, con - tra - dicts, he con - tra-
me he con - tra-dicts, he con - tra - dicts
mf
all these his sa - cred, sa - cred Gra - ces, Sears up my
con - tra-dicts all these his sa - cred Gra - ces, Sears up my lips,
-dicts all these his sa - cred Gra - ces, Sears up
all these his sa - cred Gra - ces, Sears up my lips,
lips, my eyes, my life, and from me ev - er fly - ing,
my lips, my eyes, my life, and
my lips, my eyes, my life, and from me ev - er fly - ing,
my lips, my eyes, my life, and

p
and from me ev-er fly-ing, Leads me
from me ev-er fly-ing, and from me ev-er fly-ing, Leads
ev-er fly-ing ev-er fly-ing, Leads
from me ev-er fly-ing and from me ev-er fly-ing,
in paths, leads me
me in paths, leads
me in paths, leads me in paths
Leads me in paths,
in paths, leads
me in paths, leads me in
leads me in paths, leads me in paths,
leads me in paths, leads me in paths,

me in paths, leads me in paths un-
paths, leads me in paths, leads me in paths un-
leads me in paths, leads me in paths un-tracked un-
leads me in paths, leads me in paths un-
-tracked, un-gone, and ma-ny un-couth pla-ces,
-tracked, un-gone, and ma-ny un-couth pla-ces, Where
-gone, un-gone, and ma-ny un-couth pla-ces, Where
-tracked, un-gone, and ma-ny un-couth pla-ces, Where
Where in de-
in de-spair I beau-ty curse, where in de-
in de-spair I beau-ty curse,
in de-spair I beau-ty
f

-spair, where in de - spair
-spair, where in de - spair
where in de - spair, where in de -
curse, where in de - spair I
I beau - ty curse, curse love and all
I beau - ty curse, curse love, curse love and
-spair I beau - ty curse, curse love and all
beau - ty curse, curse love and all fair
1. 2.
p
fair fa - ces. Leads me fa - ces.
all fair fa - ces. Leads fa - ces.
fair fa - ces. Leads fa - ces.
fa - ces. -ces.

No. 14. WHY DO I FRET?

fret and grieve, why do I fret
grieve, why do I fret and grieve,
fret and grieve, why do I fret and grieve,
why do I fret and grieve,
and grieve, since she de - nies, since she de -
fret and grieve, since she de - nies,
fret and grieve, since she de - nies,
fret and grieve, since she de - nies, since
p
-nies, since she de - nies, she de -
since she de - nies, since she de - nies, since
since she de - nies, since she de - -
she de - nies, since she de - nies, since she de -

* 𝅗𝅥. 𝅘𝅥 in original
E A

*This Note is misprinted E in the original edition.

will not be, and yet it will not be,
p
And yet it will not be, and yet it
be, and yet it will not be, and
mf
yet it will not be, and yet it will not
mf
and yet it will not be, and yet it will not
will not be, and yet it will not be, it will not
mf
yet it will not be, and yet it will not be, it will not
be, and yet it will not be, and yet it will not
mf
mf
be, O bit - ter, bit - ter pain,
p
be, O bit - ter, bit - ter pain, bit - ter
p
be, O bit - ter, bit - ter pain,
p
be, O bit - ter,
p
p

cresc.
mf
O bit-ter, bit-ter pain, O bit-ter, bit-ter pain,
bit-ter pain, O bit-ter, bit-ter pain, O bit-ter,
O bit-ter, bit-ter pain, O bit-ter,
bit-ter pain, O bit-ter, bit-ter pain,
p
O bit-ter, bit-ter pain, O bit-
bit-ter pain, O bit-ter, bit-ter pain, O bit-ter, bit-ter
bit-ter pain, bit-ter, bit-ter pain, O bit-ter
O bit-ter, bit-ter pain, O bit-
1.
2.
-ter, bit-ter pain. pain.
pain, bit-ter pain. Whilst pain.
pain, O bit-ter pain. pain.
-ter pain. pain.

Nº 15. ALL IN A CAVE.

Thes - ta - lis, met wan - ton Thes - ta - -
-lis, Where he un - skilled in bet - ter sports,
Thes - ta - lis, met wan - ton Thes - ta - lis, Where
-lis, met wan - ton Thes - ta - lis, Where
-lis, Where he un - skilled in bet - ter sports, begged
where he un-skilled in bet - ter, bet - ter sports,
he un-skilled in bet - - ter sports, begged on - ly
he un-skilled in bet - ter sports, begged on ly for a
on - ly for a kiss, begged on - ly for a
begged on - ly for a kiss, begged on - ly
for a kiss, begged on - ly for a kiss,
kiss, begged on - ly for a kiss,
p
mf

kiss, begged on - ly for a kiss, a kiss, a
for a kiss, begged on - ly for a kiss, a kiss, a
begged on - ly for a kiss, a kiss, a
begged on - ly for a kiss, a kiss, a
kiss, A - las, a - las, quoth she, and
kiss, A - las, a - las, quoth she, and
kiss, A - las, a - las, quoth she, and
kiss, A - las, a - las, quoth she,
take thee this, and this, and take thee
take thee this, and this, and take thee this, and this,
take thee this, and this, and take thee this, and this, and
and take thee this, and this,

p
this, and this, this and this, and take thee this, and this,
p
and take thee this, and this,
p
take thee this, and this, and take thee this, and this,
p
and take thee this, and this, and take thee
p
mf
and take thee this, and this, and this.
p
But
mf
and take thee this, and this, this and this.
p
But
mf
and take thee this, and this, this and this.
p
But
mf
p
this, and this, and take thee this, and this.
But
mf
p
know'st thou not fair Boy in love, a more con-tent-ed
know'st thou not fair Boy in love, a more con-tent-ed
know'st thou not fair Boy in love, a more con-tent-ed
know'st thou not fair Boy in love,

cresc.
sweet, a more con-tent-ed sweet, a more con-
cresc.
sweet, a more con - tent - ed sweet, a more con-
cresc.
sweet, a more con-tent-ed sweet, a more con - tent - ed sweet, a
cresc.
a more con - tent - ed sweet, a more con - tent - ed sweet, a
cresc.
mf
-tent - ed sweet, a more con - tent - ed sweet?
mf p
-tent - ed sweet, a more con - tent - ed sweet? O
mf
more con - tent - ed sweet, a more con - tent - ed sweet?
mf
more con - tent - ed sweet, a more con - tent - ed sweet?
mf
p
p
O no
no he said, O
p
O no he said, he said,
p
O no he said, O no

Heere endeth the foure Parts.

Nº 16. SING WE, DANCE WE.

Brightly in moderate time.
SOPRANO. (CANTUS.)
Sing we, dance we on the green,
SOPRANO. (ALTUS.)
Sing we, dance we on the green, and fill these val - leys,
ALTO. (TENOR.)
Sing we, dance we on the green, and fill these val - leys,
TENOR. (QUINTUS.)
Sing we, dance we on the green, and fill these val - leys,
BASS. (BASSUS.)
Sing we, dance we on the green, and
PIANOFORTE. (For rehearsal only.)
and fill these val - leys with our me - lo - dious strains,
and fill these val - leys with our me - lo - dious strains,
and fill these val - leys with our me - lo - dious strains, and
fill these val - leys with our me - lo - dious strains, and fill these
fill these val - leys, and fill these

and fill these val-leys, fill these val-leys
and fill these val - leys, val – leys, and fill these val-leys
fill these val-leys, and fill these val - leys, and fill these val-leys
val-leys with our me - lo - dious strains, and fill these val-leys
val-leys with our me - lo - dious strains, and fill these val-leys, fill these val-leys
with our me - lo - dious strains, for joy that our Sum-mer's
with our me - lo - dious strains,
with our me - lo - dious strains, for joy that our Sum-mer's
with our me - lo - dious strains, for joy that our Sum-mer's
with our me - lo - dious strains, for

Queen, that our Sum-mer's Queen, for joy that our Sum-mer's
for joy that our Sum-mer's Queen, for
Queen, that our Sum - mer's Queen, for joy that our Sum - mer's
Queen, that our Sum - mer's Queen, for joy that our Sum-mer's
joy that our Sum-mer's Queen, for joy that our Sum-mer's
Queen, that our Sum-mer's Queen, for joy that our Sum - mer's
joy that our Sum-mer's Queen, for joy that our Sum-mer's Queen, our Sum-mer's
Queen, that our Sum-mer's Queen, for joy that our Sum - mer's, Sum-mer's
Queen, for joy that our Sum - mer's
Queen, that our Sum-mer's Queen, joy that our Sum-mer's

Queen, en - vi - ron - ed, en - vi - ron - ed, en -
Queen, en - vi - ron -
Queen, en - vi - ron - ed, en - vi - ron - ed, en -
Queen, en - vi - ron - ed, en - vi - ron - ed,
Queen, en -
- vi - - ron - ed with all the coun - try swains, Fair - ly
- ed with all the coun - try swains,
- vi - - ron - ed with all the coun - try swains,
with all the coun - try swains,
- vi - - ron - ed with all the coun - try swains,

trips it o'er the plains, fair - ly trips it o'er the
Fair - ly trips it o'er the plains,
Fair - ly trips it o'er the
the coun - try swains, Fair - ly trips it o'er the plains, fair - ly
coun - try swains, Fair - ly trips it o'er the plains, o'er the
plains, fair - ly trips it o'er the plains,
fair - ly trips it o'er the plains,
plains, fair - ly trips it,
trips it o'er the plains, fair - ly trips it o'er the
plains, fair - ly trips it o'er the plains,

fair - ly trips it o'er the plains. Let us a -
fair - ly trips it o'er the plains. Let us a -
fair - ly trips it o'er the plains. Let us a -
plains, fair - ly trips it o'er the plains. Let us a -
fair - ly trips it o'er the plains. Let us a -
p
-bout, let us a - bout these Daf - fa - dil - lies sweet,
-bout, let us a - bout these Daf - fa - dil - lies sweet,
-bout, let us a - bout these Daf - fa - dil - lies sweet, let us a -
-bout, let us a - bout, let us a - bout these
-bout, let us a - bout, let us a - bout these

these Daf - fa - dil - lies
a - bout these Daf - fa - dil - lies sweet,
- bout these Daf - fa - dil - lies sweet,
Daf - fa - dil - lies sweet, these
Daf - fa - dil - lies sweet, let us a - bout these
sweet, these Daf - fa - dil - lies sweet,
a - bout these Daf - fa - dil - lies sweet,
these Daf - fa - dil - lies sweet,
Daf - fa - dil - lies sweet, Daf - fa - dil - lies sweet,
Daf - fa - dil - lies sweet, Daf - fa - dil - - lies sweet,

f
Tread a ring dance with our feet, tread a
f
Tread a ring dance with our feet, tread a
f
Tread a ring dance with our feet, tread a
f
Tread a ring dance with our feet, tread a
f
Tread a ring dance with our feet, tread a
3
f
(o. = d)
1.
2.
p
ring dance with our feet. Let us a - feet.
p
ring dance with our feet. Let us a - feet.
p
ring dance with our feet. Let us a - feet.
p
ring dance with our feet. Let us a - feet.
p
ring dance with our feet. Let us a - feet.
3
p

Nº 17. UNDER THE TOPS OF HELICON.

-con, un - der the tops of He - li -
un - der the tops of He - li - He - li
un - der the tops of He - li - con, of He - li -
- li - con, un - der the tops of He - li -
un - der the tops of He - li - con, of He - li -
- con, Not far from Par - nass' state - ly
- con, Not far from Par - nass' state - ly towers, not
- con, Not
- con, Not far from Par - nass' state - ly towers, not far from
- con, Not far from Par - nass' state - ly towers,

towers, state - ly towers, not far from Par - nass' state - ly,
far from Par - nass', not far from Par - nass'
far from Par - nass' state - ly towers, not far from Par - nass'
Par - nass' state - ly towers, from Par - nass' state - ly towers, Par -
not far from Par - nass' state - ly towers,
state - ly towers, Springs forth the foun - tain Hip - po - crene, springs
state - ly towers, Springs forth the foun - tain Hip - po - crene,
state - ly towers, Springs forth the foun - tain Hip - po - crene, springs
- nass' state - ly towers, Springs forth the foun - tain Hip - po - crene, springs
state - ly towers, Springs forth the foun - tain Hip - po - crene,

mf
forth the fountain Hip-po-crene, the fountain Hip-po-crene, springs
springs forth the fountain Hip-po-crene,
mf
forth the fountain Hip-po-crene, fountain Hip-po-crene, springs
mf
forth the fountain Hip-po-crene, springs forth the fountain
mf
fountain Hip-po-crene, springs
mf
forth the fountain Hip-po-crene, springs forth the foun-tain Hip-po-
mf
springs forth the fountain Hip-po-crene, Hip-po-
forth the fountain Hip-po-crene, the fountain Hip-po-
Hip-po-crene, the fountain Hip-po-crene the fountain Hip-po-
forth the fountain Hip-po-crene, springs forth the fountain Hip-po-

p
f
-crene, With banks be - set with fra - grant flowers, with
-crene, With banks be - set with fra - grant flowers, with
-crene, With banks be - set with fra - grant flowers, with
-crene, With banks be - set with fra - grant flowers, with
-crene, With banks be - set with fra - grant flowers, with
banks be - set with fra - grant flowers. The
banks be - set with fra - grant flowers. The
banks be - set with fra - grant flowers. The
fra - grant flowers, be - set with fra - grant flowers.
banks be - set with fra - grant flowers.

hill is it, the hill is it my Mu - ses use, is
hill is it my Mu - ses use, my Mu - ses_ use, the hill is
hill is it my Mu - ses use, my Mu - ses use, the hill is
The hill is it my
it my Mu - ses use, the hill is it my Mu - ses use,
mf
it my Mu - ses use, the hill is
it my Mu - ses use, the hill is it my Mu - ses use,
Mu - ses use, the hill is it my Mu - ses use,
mf
The hill is it my Mu - ses, Mu - ses use, the
mf

mf
p
the hill is it my Mu - ses use, my Mu - ses use, The
it my Mu - ses use, my Mu - ses use, The
the hill is it my Mu - ses use, The
the hill is it my Mu - ses use, my Mu - ses use, The
hill is it my Mu - ses use, my Mu - ses use, The
1.
2.
foun - tain which my heart doth choose. The choose.
foun - tain which my heart doth choose. The choose.
foun - tain which my heart doth choose. The choose.
foun tain which my heart doth choose. choose.
foun - tain which my heart doth choose. choose.

Nº 18. SWEET PHILLIDA.

mf
-da, my flocks as white and pure as
Phil - li - da, my flocks as white and pure as
-da, my flocks as white and pure as
my flocks as white and pure as
-da, my flocks as white and pure as
snow - y down, my flocks as white and pure as snow - y
snow - y, snow - y down, my
snow - y down, my flocks as white and pure as snow - y
snow - y down, my flocks as white and pure as snow - y
snow - y down, my

down, my flocks as white and pure,
flocks as white and pure, my
down, my flocks as white and pure, my
down, my flocks as white and pure, my flocks as white and
flocks as white and pure, my flocks as white and pure, my
my flocks as white and pure as snow - y down,
flocks as white and pure as snow - y down,
flocks as white and pure as snow - y down,
pure, my flocks as white and pure as snow - y down, sit
flocks as white and pure as snow - y down, sit
p
p
p

p
sit mourn - ing for thy sake,
p
sit mourn - ing for thy sake,
p
sit mourn ing for thy
mourn - ing for thy sake, thy sake, sit
mourn - ing for thy sake, sit mourn - ing
sit mourm - - ing for thy sake, sit
for thy sake, sit mourn - - ing for
sake, for thy sake, sit
mourn - ing for thy sake, sit mourn - - ing for
for thy sake, thy sake,

mourn - ing for thy sake, sit mourn - ing
thy sake, sit mourn - ing for thy
mourn - ing for thy sake, sit
thy sake, sit mourn - ing for thy sake, thy
sit mourn - ing for thy
for thy sake, for thy sake.
sake, sit mourn - ing for thy sake.
mourn - ing for thy sake, thy sake.
sake, sit mourn - ing for thy sake thy sake.
sake, sit mourn - ing for thy sake.

* G is possibly a misprint for B.
† faulty underlay

*C natural may be sung here if the effect is thought too harsh.

p
mf
will par - take. Come quick-ly, come quick-ly, come quick-ly,
will par - take. Come quick-ly, come quick-ly, come
will par - take. Come quick-ly, come quick-ly, come
take, par - take. Come quick-ly, come quick-ly, come
will par - take. Come quick-ly, come quick-ly, come
come quick-ly, come, come, come, I sigh,
quick-ly, come quick-ly, come, come, I sigh, I
quick-ly, come quick-ly, come, come, I sigh, I
quick-ly, come quick-ly, come, come, I sigh, I
quick-ly, come quick-ly, come, come, I sigh, I

p
mf
I sigh for thee my dear - est
sigh, I sigh for thee my dear - est
sigh, I sigh for thee my dear - est
sigh, I sigh for thee my dear - est
sigh, I sigh for thee my dear - est
cresc.
sweet, I'll turn my flocks a - way, I'll turn my
sweet, I'll turn my flocks a - way, I'll turn my
sweet, I'll turn my flocks a - way, I'll turn my
sweet, I'll turn my flocks a - way, I'll turn my
sweet, I'll turn my flocks a - way, I'll turn my

mf
(o. = d)
flocks a - way, And with them I'll not stay,
flocks a - way, And with them I'll not stay, So
flocks a - way, And with them I'll not stay,
flocks a - way, And with them I'll not stay,
flocks a - way, And with them I'll not stay,
So thee and I most lov - ing - ly,
thee and I most lov - ing - ly, so thee and I most
So thee and I most lov - ing - ly, lov - ing - ly,
So thee and I most lov - ing - ly, so
So thee and I most lov - ing - ly,

p
so thee and I most lov - ing -
lov - ing - ly,
so
lov - ing - ly, so thee and I most lov - ing - ly, lov - ing -
thee and I most lov - ing - ly, so thee and I most
so thee and I most lov - ing, lov - ing - ly,
- ly, so thee and I most lov - ing - ly, in
thee and I most lov - ing - ly, so thee and I in
- ly, so thee and I most lov - ing - ly,
lov - ing - ly, lov - ing - ly, lov - ing - ly, in
so thee and I most lov - ing, lov - ing - ly,

cresc.
love each o - ther meet, in love each o - ther
cresc.
love each o - ther meet, in love each o - ther
cresc.
each o - ther meet, o - ther
cresc.
love each o - ther meet, in love each o - ther
cresc.
each o - ther meet, o - ther
cresc.
f
meet, in love each o - ther meet.
f
meet, in love each o - ther meet.
f
meet, in love each o - - ther meet.
f
meet, in love each o - - - ther meet.
f
meet, in love each o - ther meet.
f

Nº 19. MY HEART IS DEAD.

Two moderate beats in a bar.

dead with - in me, my heart is
me, my heart is dead with - in me,
- in me, my
my heart is dead with - in me, is
- in me, my
dead, is dead with - in me, For that my
my heart is dead with - in me, For that my
heart is dead with - in me, For that my
dead with - in me, For that my love for -
heart is dead with - in me, For that my

mf
love for - sakes me, Yet why should I,
love for - sakes me, Yet why should I, yet why should
love for - sakes me, Yet
-sakes me, for - sakes me, Yet why should I
love for - sakes me,
yet why should I shed tears, shed tears in vain? shed
I shed tears in vain? yet why should I shed
why should I shed tears in vain? shed tears
shed tears in vain? shed tears in vain?
Yet why should I, yet why should I shed

tears in vain? shed tears in
tears in vain? shed tears in
in vain?
yet why should I shed tears in
tears in vain? yet why should I shed tears in
vain? yet why should I shed tears in vain?
vain? yet why should I shed tears in vain? yet
yet why should I shed tears in vain? yet
vain? yet why should I shed tears in vain? yet
vain? yet why should I shed tears in vain?

shed tears in vain? yet why should I
why should I shed tears in vain? shed
why should I shed tears in vain? yet why should I
why should I shed tears in vain?
yet why should I
shed tears in vain? shed tears in vain? She will not
tears in vain shed tears in vain? She will not once
shed tears in vain? shed tears in vain? She will not
yet why should I shed tears in vain? She will not
shed tears in vain? shed tears in vain? She will not

*This note is printed B in the repeat in the original edition.

there - fore will joy, sing and dance, I
joy, sing and dance, I there - fore will
dance, I there - fore will joy, sing and dance, I
dance, sing and dance, I there - fore will,
dance, sing and dance, I there - fore will joy, sing and
there-fore will joy, I there-fore will joy, sing and dance, In
joy, sing and dance, joy, sing and dance, In
there - fore will joy, sing and dance, joy, sing and dance, In
I there-fore will joy sing and dance, sing and dance,
dance, sing and dance, I there - fore will joy, sing and dance, In
p
3/4

f
hope to cast a bet - ter chance, in hope to
hope to cast a bet - ter chance, in hope to
hope to cast a bet - ter chance, in hope to
p
joy, sing and dance, In hope to
hope to cast a bet - ter chance, in hope to
1.
2.
cast a bet - ter chance, a bet - ter chance. I chance.
cast a bet - ter, a bet - ter chance. chance.
cast a bet - ter chance, a bet - ter chance. chance.
cast a bet - ter chance, a bet - ter chance. I chance.
cast a bet - ter chance, a bet - ter chance. chance.

Nº 20. NO, NO, IT WILL NOT BE.

no, it will not be, Your la - bour is in
no, it will not be, Your la - bour is in
no, no, no, no, no, it will not be, Your la - bour is in
no, no, no, no, it will not be, Your la-bour is in
no, no, no, no, no, it will not be, Your la - bour is in
mf
vain, I stay you not,
vain, I stay you not, I
vain, I stay you not, I
vain, I stay you not, I stay you
vain, I stay you not,

f
I stay you not, I stay you not, but
f
stay you not, but set you free,
stay you not, I stay you not, I stay you not,
f
not, I stay you not, I stay you not, but
f
I stay you not, I stay you not, but
f
f
set you free, but set you free, but
but set you free,
f
but set you, set you free,
set you free, set you free, set
set you free, but set you free, set you free, but set you

set you free, but_ set you free, but set you
but set you free, but set you free, but set_ you
but set you free,_ but set you
_ you free, but set_ you free, but set you
free, set_ you free, set you, set you free, but set you
p
free, Why do you then com - plain, why do you
p
free, Why do you then com - plain,
p
free, Why do you then com - plain, and wail con -
p
free, Why do you then com - plain,
p
free, Why do you then com - plain,
p

then com - plain, And wail con - ceit - ed
And wail con - ceit - ed wrongs, and wail con-ceit-ed
-ceit - ed wrongs? con - ceit - ed wrongs, and wail con - ceit - ed
And wail con - ceit - ed wrongs? and
And wail con -
wrongs? and wail con - ceit - ed wrongs? and
wrongs, and wail con - ceit - ed wrongs? and
wrongs? and wail con - ceit -
wail con - ceit - ed wrongs? con - ceit - ed wrongs? and
-ceit - ed wrongs? and wail con -

wail con - ceit - ed wrongs? and wail con -
wail con - ceit - ed wrongs? and wail con - ceit - ed
- ed wrongs? and wail con-ceit - ed wrongs?
wail con - ceit - ed wrongs? and wail con - ceit -
- ceit - ed, con - ceit - ed wrongs? and wail and
- ceit - ed wrongs? and wail con - ceit - ed wrongs, con -
wrongs as done to me?
and wail con - ceit - ed wrongs, con -
- ed wrongs? and wail con -
wail con - ceit - ed wrongs as done to

mf
-ceit - ed wrongs as done to me? No, no, no, no, no,
con-ceit-ed wrongs as done to me? No, no, no, no, no,
-ceit - ed wrongs as done to me? No, no, no, no, no,
-ceit - ed wrongs as done to me? No, no, no, no, no,
f
me, as done to me? No, no, no, no, no,
no, no, no, no, no, I tell you once a - gain, I
no, no, no, no, no, I tell you once a - gain,
no, no, no, no, no, I tell you once a -
no, no, no, no, no, no, no, no, no, I
no, no, no, no, no, no, no, no, no, no, I tell you once a -

tell you once a - gain, I tell you once a -
I tell you once a-gain, I tell you once a -
-gain, I tell you once a - gain, I tell you once a -
tell you once a - gain, I tell you once a - gain,
-gain, I tell you once a-gain, I
p
p
p
p
-gain, I tell you once a-gain, I tell you once a - gain, I
-gain, I tell you once a-gain, I tell you once a - gain, I
-gain, I tell you once a-gain, I tell you once a-gain, I
I tell you once a - gain, I tell you once a-gain, I
tell you once a - gain, I tell you once a-gain, I
mf
mf
mf
mf
mf
mf

tell you once a - gain, You have your tra - vail for your
tell you once a - gain, I tell you once a - gain, You have your
tell you once a - gain, You have your tra - vail for your pain,
tell you once a - gain, You have your tra - vail for your pain, you
tell you once a - gain, You have your tra - vail for your pain,
pain, your tra - vail for your pain, for your pain.
tra - vail for your pain, for your pain.
your tra - vail for your pain, for your pain.
have your tra - vail for your pain, for your pain.
for your pain.

※The original edition has a crotchet rest but in the repeat it is correctly printed as a minim.

f
will not — be, no, no, no, no, no, it
no, no, no, no, no, no, it — will not be, —
no, it will not — be, no, no, no, no, no,
f
no, it will not be, no, no, no, it
f
no, it will not — be, no, no, it
f
f
will not be. be.
1. 2.
f
— it will not be. be.
f
it will — not — be. be.
will not — be, not be. be.
will not be. be.

No. 21. WHEN ORIANA WALKED.

cresc.
O - ri - an - a walked to take the air, the world did strive, the
O - ri - an - a walked to take the air, the world did strive, the
O - ri - an - a walked to take the air, the world did strive, the
take the air, to take the air, the world did strive, the
O - ri - an - a walked to take the air, the world did strive, the
f
world did strive to en - ter - tain so fair, to en - ter - tain so
world did strive to en - ter - tain so fair, to en - ter - tain so
world did strive to en - ter - tain so fair, to en - ter - tain so fair,
world did strive to en - ter - tain so fair, to en - ter - tain so
world did strive to en - ter - tain so fair, to en - ter - tain so

p
fair, By Flo - ra fair, by
p
fair, By Flo - ra fair,
p
By Flo - ra fair and sweet-est flowers, by
p
fair, By Flo - ra fair and sweet - est flowers,
fair,
p
Flo - ra fair and sweet - est flowers, by Flo - ra fair and
by Flo - ra fair, by Flo - ra fair and
Flo - ra fair and sweet - est flowers, sweet - est flowers,
and sweet - est flowers, and sweet - est flowers, and

mf
sweet - est flowers were strewn, by Flo - ra fair and sweet - est flowers,
mf
sweet - est flowers were strewn, by Flo - ra fair and sweet - est flowers,
mf
sweet - est flowers were strewn, by Flo - ra fair and sweet - est flowers,
mf
sweet - est flowers were strewn, by Flo - ra fair and sweet - est flowers,
mf
by Flo - ra fair and sweet - est flowers,
mf
sweet - est flowers were strewn, A - long the way, a - long the way,
sweet - est flowers were strewn, A - long the way for her,
sweet - est flowers were strewn, A - long the way, a - long the
sweet - est flowers were strewn, A - long the way for her to tread up - on,
sweet - est flowers were strewn, A - long,

a - long the way for her to tread up - on, for her to
for her to tread up - on, for her to tread up -
way, a - long the way for her, for
a - long the way for her to tread, for
a - long the way for her to
tread up - on, The trees did blos - som, the sil - ver riv - ers
-on, to tread up - on, The trees did blos - som,
her to tread up - on, The trees did blos - som,
her to tread up - on, The trees did blos - som, the sil - ver
tread up - on, The trees did blos - som,

ran, the sil - ver riv - ers ran, the sil - ver riv - ers
the sil - ver riv - ers ran, the sil - ver, sil - ver riv - ers
the sil - ver riv - ers ran, The
riv - ers, sil - ver riv - ers ran, The
the sil - ver riv - ers ran, the sil - ver riv - ers ran,
ran, The wind did gen - tly play up - on her
ran, The wind did gen - tly play, did gen - tly play up - on her
wind did gen - tly play up - on her
wind did gen - tly play up - on her
The wind did gen - tly play up - on her

fan, And then for to de - light her Gra-ce's ear,
fan, And then for to de - light her Gra-ce's ear,
cresc.
fan, And then for to de-light,
cresc.
fan, And then for to de-light,
cresc.
fan, And then for to de - light her Gra-ce's ear, And
cresc.
mf
The woods a Tem-ple seemed, the woods a Tem-ple
mf
The woods a Tem-ple seemed, the woods a Tem-ple
f
to de-light her Gra - ce's ear, The woods a Tem-ple
f
to de-light her Gra - ce's ear, her Gra-ce's ear, The woods a Tem-ple
f
then for to de - light her Gra - ce's ear, The woods a Tem-ple
mf
f

(𝅗𝅥 = 𝅝.)
f
seemed, the Birds a Choir, Then sang the shep-herds and
seemed, the Birds a Choir, Then sang the shep-herds and
seemed, the Birds a Choir, Then sang the shep-herds and
seemed, the Birds a Choir, Then sang the shep-herds and
seemed, the Birds a Choir, Then sang the shep-herds and
(𝅝. = 𝅗𝅥)
Nymphs of Di - an - a, in heaven lives
Nymphs of Di - an - a, in heaven lives
Nymphs of Di - an - a, in heaven, in heaven
Nymphs of Di - an - a,
Nymphs of Di - an - a, in heaven lives

O - ri - an - a,
O - ri - an - a, in heaven
lives O - ri - an - a, in
in heaven lives O - ri - an - a, in heaven lives
O - ri - an - a, in heaven lives
in heaven lives O - ri - an - a,
lives O - ri - an - a, in heaven
heaven lives O - ri - an - a, in heaven
O - ri - an - a, in
O - - ri - an - a, O - ri -

In heaven, in
lives O - ri - an - a, lives O - ri -
lives O - ri - an - a,
heaven lives O - ri - an - a, in heaven lives
- an - a, in heaven lives O - ri -
heaven lives O - ri - an - a, in
p
- an - a, in heaven lives O - ri - an - a,
in heaven lives O - ri - an - a,
O - ri - an - a, lives fair O - ri - an - a,
- an - a, O - ri - an - a, in
p
p

heaven lives O - ri - an - a, in heaven lives O - ri - an -
in heaven lives O - ri - an - a, in
in
in heaven lives O - ri - an - a, in heaven lives
heaven lives O - ri - an - a, in heaven lives O - ri - an -
- a, in heaven lives O - ri - an -
heaven lives O - ri - an - a, in heaven lives O - ri -
heaven lives O - ri - an - a, in heaven lives O - ri -
O - ri - an - a, in heaven lives O - ri - an -
- a, in heaven lives O - ri - an - a, in

* E in the original edition is clearly a misprint for G.

No. 22. NOW I SEE THOU FLOUTEST ME.

*A in the original edition may be a misprint either for F or B.

p
on Clo - ris head I'll set it, on Clo - ris head I'll
p
set it, on Clo - ris head I'll set it,
p
it, on Clo - ris head I'll set it, on Clo - ris head I'll
p
set it, on Clo - ris head I'll set it, on
p
on Clo - ris head I'll set it,
p
f
set it, on Clo - ris head I'll
cresc.
f
on Clo - ris head I'll set it, on Clo - ris head I'll
cresc.
f
set it, on Clo - ris head I'll set it, on Clo - ris head I'll
cresc.
f
Clo - ris head, on Clo - ris head I'll set it, on Clo - ris head I'll
cresc.
f
on Clo - ris head I'll set it, on Clo - ris head I'll
cresc.
f

mf
set it, For her I'll ga - ther dain - ty po - sies, of
set it, For her I'll ga - ther dain - ty po - sies, of
set it, For her I'll ga - ther dain - ty po - sies, of
set it, For her I'll ga - ther dain - ty po - sies, dain - ty
set it, For her I'll ga - ther dain - ty po - sies,
Gil - ly-flowers and pur - ple Ro - ses,
Gil - ly-flowers and pur - ple Ro - ses, of Gil - ly-flowers and
Gil - ly-flowers and pur - ple Ro - ses, of Gil - ly-flowers
po - sies, of
of Gil - ly-flowers and

of Gil - ly flowers and pur - ple Ro - ses, pur - ple
pur - ple Ro - ses, of Gil - ly-flowers and pur - ple
and pur - ple Ro - ses,
Gil - ly flowers and pur - ple Ro - ses, of Gil - ly-flowers and pur - ple
pur - ple. Ro - ses, of Gil - ly-flowers and pur - ple Ro - ses,
Ro - ses, of Gil - ly-flowers and pur - ple Ro - ses, pur-ple Ro-ses.
Ro - ses, of Gil - ly-flowers and pur-ple Ro - ses, pur - ple Ro-ses.
of Gil - ly-flowers and pur - ple Ro - ses, of Gil - ly-flowers and pur - ple Ro-ses.
Ro - ses, of Gil - ly-flowers and pur-ple Ro - ses, pur-ple Ro-ses.
of Gil - ly-flowers and pur - ple Ro - ses, of Gil - ly-flowers and pur-ple Ro-ses.

f
With her on each ho-li - day, with her on each
With her on each ho - li - ho - li - day, with her on each ho - li-day,
With her on each ho - li - day, with her on each ho - li - day,
With her on each ho - li - day, with her on each
With her on each ho - li - day, with her on each ho - li - day,
ho - li - day, ho - li - day,
with her on each ho - li - day, I'll dance the
with her on each ho - li - day, I'll dance the mer - ry
ho - li - day, ho - li - day, I'll
ho - li - day, I'll dance the mer - ry, mer - ry

I'll dance the mer-ry, mer-ry roun - de - lay,
mer-ry, mer-ry roun - de - lay, I'll dance the mer-ry, mer-ry
roun - de-lay, I'll dance the mer-ry, mer-ry roun - de -
dance the mer-ry, mer-ry roun - de-lay, I'll dance the
roun - de-lay, I'll dance the mer-ry, mer-ry
I'll dance the mer-ry, mer-ry roun - de-lay, I'll
roun - de-lay, I'll dance the mer-ry, mer-ry
-lay, I'll dance the mer-ry, mer-ry roun - de-lay,
mer-ry, mer-ry roun-de - lay, I'll dance the mer-ry, mer-ry
roun - de-lay, I'll dance the mer-ry, mer-ry roun - de -

dance the mer - ry, mer - ry roun - de - roun - de - lay, And
roun - de - lay, the mer - ry roun - de - lay, And
roun - de - lay, the mer - ry, mer - ry roun - de - lay, And
roun - de - lay, mer - ry roun - de - lay,
-lay, the mer - ry, mer - ry roun - de - lay,
this I know will move thee, and this I know will
this I know will move thee, this I know will
this I know will move thee, and this I know will

*♮ in original

Lowe and Brydone (Printers) Limited, London

INDEX

JACOBEAN CONSORT MUSIC

EDITED BY

THURSTON DART AND WILLIAM COATES

			Score s. d.	Each Part
1.	FANTASIA *à* 3 .. .. Viol Consort or String Trio	Giovanni Coperario	1 0	6d.
2.	FANTASIA *à* 4 .. .. .. ALMAN *à* 4 .. .. .. Viol Consort or String Quartet	John Ward Thomas Tomkins	1 0	6d.
3.	FANTASIA *à* 4 .. .. .. Viol Consort or String Quartet	John Ward	1 0	6d.
4.	FANTASIA *à* 4 .. .. .. Viol Consort or String Quartet	Thomas Lupo	1 0	6d.
5.	FANTASIA *à* 4 .. Viol Consort or String Quartet	Alfonso Ferrabosco II	1 0	6d.
6.	FANTASIA *à* 5 .. .. Viol Consort (2 Tenors) or String Quintet (2 Violas)	Giovanni Coperario	1 0	6d.
7.	IN NOMINE *à* 5 .. .. Viol Consort (2 Tenors) or String Quintet (2 Violas)	Orlando Gibbons	1 0	6d.
8.	FOUR-NOTE PAVAN *à* 5 .. FOUR-NOTE PAVAN *à* 5 Viol Consort (2 Tenors) or String Quintet (2 Violas)	Daniel Farrant Alfonso Ferrabosco II	1 0	6d.
9.	TWO DANCES { *Male-Content* / *Alman* } String Quartet (or String Orchestra), Harpsichord (or Piano)	Thomas Simpson	1 0	6d.
10.	PAVAN .. .. BONNY SWEET ROBIN String Quartet (or String Orchestra), Harpsichord (or Piano)	John Dowland Thomas Simpson	2 0	9d.
11.	TWO SUITES .. .. Violin, Bass Viol (or Cello), Organ (or Harpsichord, or Piano)	Giovanni Coperario	2 0	9d.
12.	PASSAMEZZO PAVAN .. .. String Orchestra	Peter Phillips	2 0	9d.

These pieces have been selected from Volume IX of *Musica Britannica*; this volume also contains introductory notes and critical commentary. All suggestions of tempo, dynamics, bowing and phrasing are editorial. Printed by permission of The Royal Musical Association.

LONDON:

STAINER & BELL, LTD.

Made in Great Britain

The English School of Lutenist Song Writers

Edited by EDMUND H. FELLOWES.

JOHN BARTLET.

THOMAS CAMPIAN.

MICHAEL CAVENDISH.

JOHN ATTEY.

STAINER & BELL. LTD
29 NEWMAN STREET, LONDON. W.1
MADE IN ENGLAND

The English School of Lutenist Song Writers

Edited by EDMUND H. FELLOWES.

JOHN DOWLAND.

Awake sweet love, thou art returned
Clear or cloudy
Come again sweet love
Fine knacks for ladies
His golden locks
Say love, if ever thou did'st find

THOMAS FORD.

Now I see thy looks were feigned
Since first I saw your face }
There is a Lady sweet and kind }

ROBERT JONES.

As I the seely fish deceive
Cynthia, Queen of Seas and Lands
Do not, O do not prize
In Sherwood lived stout Robin Hood
Love is a pretty frenzy
Love is a bable
Love's god is a boy
Now what is love
Now have I Learned *DUET*
Since first disdain began to rise *DUET*
Sweet Kate *DUET*

PHILIP ROSSETER.

When Laura smiles

FRANCIS PILKINGTON.

Diaphenia

STAINER & BELL LTD
29 Newman Street, London. W.1
MADE IN ENGLAND

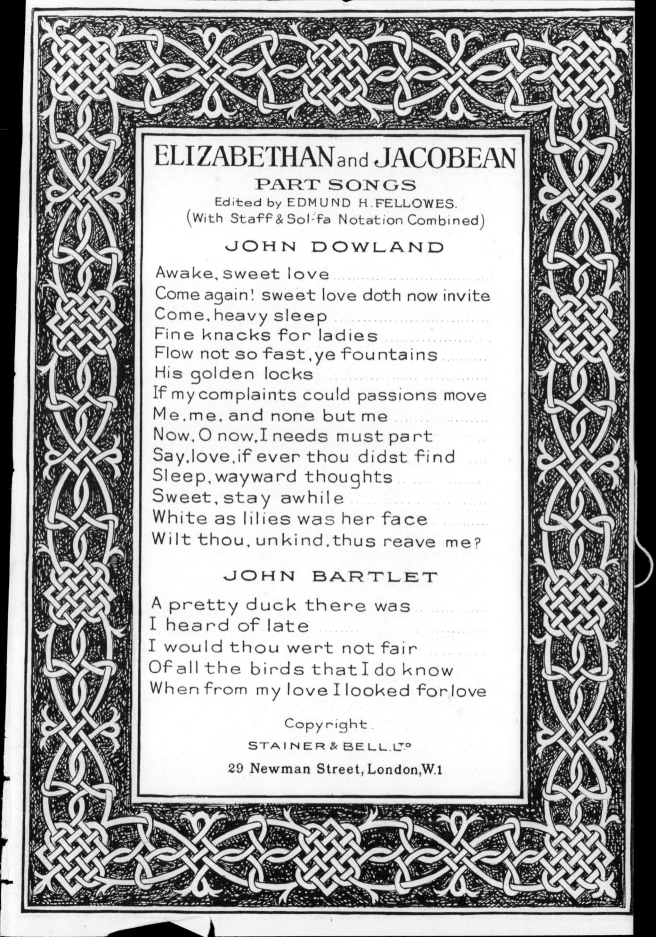

ELIZABETHAN and JACOBEAN
PART SONGS

Edited by EDMUND H. FELLOWES.
(With Staff & Sol-fa Notation Combined)

JOHN DOWLAND

Awake, sweet love
Come again! sweet love doth now invite
Come, heavy sleep
Fine knacks for ladies
Flow not so fast, ye fountains
His golden locks
If my complaints could passions move
Me, me, and none but me
Now, O now, I needs must part
Say, love, if ever thou didst find
Sleep, wayward thoughts
Sweet, stay awhile
White as lilies was her face
Wilt thou, unkind, thus reave me?

JOHN BARTLET

A pretty duck there was
I heard of late
I would thou wert not fair
Of all the birds that I do know
When from my love I looked for love

STAINER & BELL. L^TD
29 Newman Street, London, W.1

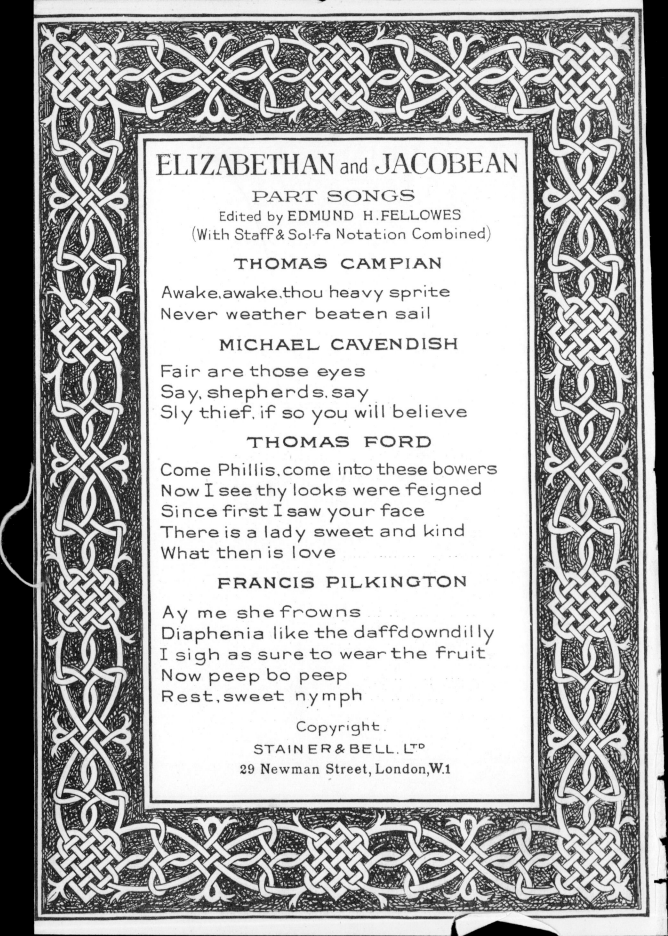

ELIZABETHAN and JACOBEAN

PART SONGS

Edited by EDMUND H. FELLOWES
(With Staff & Sol-fa Notation Combined)

THOMAS CAMPIAN

Awake, awake, thou heavy sprite
Never weather beaten sail

MICHAEL CAVENDISH

Fair are those eyes
Say, shepherds, say
Sly thief, if so you will believe

THOMAS FORD

Come Phillis, come into these bowers
Now I see thy looks were feigned
Since first I saw your face
There is a lady sweet and kind
What then is love

FRANCIS PILKINGTON

Ay me she frowns
Diaphenia like the daffdowndilly
I sigh as sure to wear the fruit
Now peep bo peep
Rest, sweet nymph

STAINER & BELL. L^TD
29 Newman Street, London, W.1